Jeremy Hooker was born in 1941 and is a poet, critic, teacher and broadcaster. He has published ten collections of poetry, of which the most recent are *Our Lady of Europe* (Enitharmon, 1997) and *Adamah* (Enitharmon, 2002). His other books include *Writers in a Landscape*, *Imagining Wales: a View of Modern Welsh Writing in English*, studies of David Jones and John Cowper Powys, and *Welsh Journal*. He has edited writings by Alun Lewis, Frances Bellerby, Richard Jefferies, Wilfred Owen, and a selection of short stories by Edward Thomas, *The Ship of Swallows*. Jeremy Hooker has taught in universities in Wales, England, the Netherlands and the USA and is currently Professor of English at the University of Glamorgan.

Jeremy Hooker

The Cut of the Light

POEMS 1965–2005

ENITHARMON PRESS

First published in 2006
by Enitharmon Press
26B Caversham Road
London NW5 2DU

www.enitharmon.co.uk

Distributed in the UK by
Central Books
99 Wallis Road
London E9 5LN

Distributed in the USA and Canada
by Dufour Editions Inc.
PO Box 7, Chester Springs
PA 19425, USA

ISBN 1 904634 27 3 (hardback)

The publisher acknowledges the financial support
of the Welsh Books Council

British Library Cataloguing-in-Publication Data.
A catalogue record for this book is available
from the British Library.

Typeset in Caslon by Servis Filmsetting Ltd, Manchester
and printed in England by
Antony Rowe Ltd

ACKNOWLEDGEMENTS

The poems in this collection first appeared (some in earlier versions) in the following books: *Soliloquies of a Chalk Giant* (Enitharmon, 1974), *Solent Shore* (Carcanet, 1978), *Itchen Water* (Winchester School of Art Press, 1982), *Master of the Leaping Figures* (Enitharmon, 1987), *Their Silence a Language* (Enitharmon, 1993), *Our Lady of Europe* (Enitharmon, 1997), *Adamah* (Enitharmon, 2002), *Arnolds Wood* (Flarestack Publishing, 2005). The first section, 'Landscape of the Daylight Moon', draws upon poems included in the anthology *Poetry Introduction 1* (Faber, 1969), and my collections *The Elements* (Christopher Davies, 1969) and *Landscape of the Daylight Moon* (Enitharmon, 1978). 'Poems to Carol' is previously unpublished. 'Passages' and 'Under Mynydd Bach' originally appeared in *Englishman's Road* (Carcanet, 1980). 'Leaving' was first published in *Common Ground: Poets in a Welsh Landscape*, ed. Susan Butler (Poetry Wales Press, 1985). I would like to express my thanks to the publishers of all of these.

BIBLIOGRAPHY

Poetry

The Elements, Christopher Davies, 1972
Soliloquies of a Chalk Giant, Enitharmon Press, 1974
Landscape of the Daylight Moon, Enitharmon Press, 1978
Solent Shore, Carcanet Press, 1978
Englishman's Road, Carcanet Press, 1980
A View from the Source, Carcanet Press, 1982
Itchen Water (with Norman Ackroyd), Winchester School of Art Press, 1982
Master of the Leaping Figures, Enitharmon Press, 1987
Their Silence a Language (with Lee Grandjean), Enitharmon Press, 1993
Our Lady of Europe, Enitharmon Press, 1997
Groundwork (with Lee Grandjean), Djanogly Art Gallery, 1998
Adamah, Enitharmon Press, 2002
Arnolds Wood, Flarestack, 2005
Reflections on Ground and Seventeen Poems, Free Poetry, 2005

Prose

John Cowper Powys, University of Wales Press, 1973
David Jones: An Exploratory Study, Enitharmon Press, 1975
John Cowper Powys and David Jones: A Comparative Study, Enitharmon Press, 1979
Poetry of Place, Carcanet Press, 1982
The Presence of the Past: Essays on British and American Poetry, Poetry Wales Press, 1987
Writers in a Landscape, University of Wales Press, 1996
Imagining Wales: A View of Modern Welsh Writing in English, University of Wales Press, 2001
Welsh Journal, Seren, 2001

Editions

Poems '71, Gwasg Gomer, 1971

Selected Poems of Alun Lewis (with Gweno Lewis), Allen and Unwin, 1981

Selected Stories by Frances Bellerby, Enitharmon Press, 1986

Inwards Where All The Battle Is: Writings from India by Alun Lewis, Gregynog Press, 1997

At Home on the Earth: A new selection of the later writings of Richard Jefferies, Green Books, 2001

Edward Thomas, *The Ship of Swallows,* Enitharmon Press, 2005

CONTENTS

from SOLILOQUIES OF A CHALK GIANT
(Enitharmon Press, 1974)

from **SOLENT SHORE** (Carcanet Press, 1978)

from **ENGLISHMAN'S ROAD** (Carcanet Press, 1980)

1 **Passages**

2 **Under Mynydd Bach**

13

from **OUR LADY OF EUROPE** (Enitharmon Press, 1997)

1   **A Troy of the North**

from
LANDSCAPE OF THE DAYLIGHT MOON
1965–73

TENCH FISHER'S DAWN

We are before dawn intruders,
Mesmerised by the quizzical pitch eye
Of the lake's animal presence.
It swallows our words without a ripple,
And where we crept up the grasses
Uncoil, effacing our prints. The close dark
Isolates our human stink like prey.
But when the stars melt out and dawn
Unsheathes the black acres, and the water
Pales, steaming under the risen sun,
We can see the bubbles cluster and burst.
Then, casting out, we're suddenly in touch.

POEMS TO CAROL

Listening to Silence

I think often of silence
And put my ear to it
                    straining to hear
What breathes or what it is that listens.
Take, for example, the pause
                    smelling damply of stone
Before a Bach fugue builds.
                    Or the stillness
When the clouds are bruised blue-black.
There are moments at parties and in cities,
Where, when the noise is loudest
I am blinded to all but silence
                    becoming visible,
Black-capped, chalk-white . . .
Between us

21

                              there are times
                                          when I touch an arm
And do not know if it is yours
                                                  or mine.

Those I fear most
Are when, as you say, my words drum
Like hail on a tin roof
And I become
                    speechless as an idiot with a book
Watching you watch them melt.

Loving you, I loved this place

Loving you, I loved this place,
Was, in your absence, most content alone
And dreaming in the silence of the hills
A future legendary as the past.
                                          Remember
How I hurried back to write of buzzards
Mewing in the sky; was startled by blood–
Berried rowans into praise, and told you
How the gale had made the cherry groan?
And telling you I was at home.

But now the place is changed: you won't return.
I am the perfect stranger come at last
To this essential solitude. Tonight
The wind sounds baffled in the hills;
It makes the silence bottomless.

Into it I drop the one word, 'love'

Cwm Morgan

Once in late summer
Through oakleaves darkened by an autumn breath
I glimpsed the falling river

Torn to shreds of foam, and fancied
That one fleck of whiteness swiftly gone
Might be the fleeting silk
Of an enchantress in your tales.
Then as I turned away
You smiled, as if to say
Cwm Morgan was your gift to me.
                    I did not know
The autumn was already come
When you would slip from me like foam.

Springing

'It's springing', you said. Yes,
And our quickened senses affirmed
New life breaking the mould, love
Rediscovering our wintered selves.
And we were glad, as all must be,
Whatever cruelty has been done,
Disaster undergone, from spring to spring.
Nor could we then foresee
Another separate wintering.

THOMAS HARDY BURNING LETTERS

Commonsense does it.
First, bed it down, then rake over
Dry grass, dry sticks: that's the knack –
You don't know there's a breeze
Till it snatches; not too tight, though,
Or the match won't take.
That's it.
          Now the paper blackens,
Wrinkles like dead leaves, stains red
As the flames worm through.
It catches. And the heart blooms. Blooms,

And fails into smoke. The ash settles,
And you die as it dies, consumed.
There's only a pale film left, more delicate than petals.

They're all at it, gumbooted, sentinel,
Forking on weeds, trash, contents of attics.
You can see smoke standing up all over Wessex.

Here's a man
Has a face only the mirror knows,
Who's watched himself burn there
And outstared the horror.
His pitiless scorched lip twitches.
I wonder, is that for a word
The fire glowed through
Before the heart crumpled,
Or because he sees
Scholars, years after,
Scrabble for ash on their knees?

STRATA FLORIDA ABBEY
(The burial place of Dafydd ap Gwilym)

Dafydd ap Gwilym is earth.
A dandy ogling girls in church;
They redden, flush with laughter
As a gargoyle holds its mirth.
The priest's eye drips like rain . . .
And always gulls are crying
With a voice no girl can still,
As if he'd taught them how to yearn.
He worded it: such foolishness,
Such craving as heart put him to,
But took what offered, uttering all:
The pageant and the promise of his time
When princes honoured him

24

Who now are underfoot and crumbled
With the monks and soldiery.

        And not a pinch of blood remains
Except the blood-red stalks
With which herb robert grips the corpse-grey stones
That even tender hart's-tongue ferns have pierced.
I watch a wagtail's pulsing throat;
It's nesting in the sacristy.
There's so much sky. One arch alone survives.
        The guide is seventy
He tells us, pausing by an abbot's tomb;
Retires next year. My father, too.
The group moves down the grassy nave.
I stay to trace the fading Celtic cross,
Then, fingers grey with dust, I turn
But stop like one caught robbing graves.
The blood pricks sharper in my veins
To see my parents stand, heads bowed,
Attentive to that distant history.

What's that to us? It was so long ago
And yet, once dead and out of time,
We are as old. The minutes pass
And as I write they pass and as you read.
I want no kin with stone nor monument,
Unless for dusty hands that lifted them
For bird and plant to repossess.
And knowing this, that time is sure
To turn our homes to graves, then rifle them,
To walk in ruins startles me to love
Those unique hands that break
The sky's monotony and build in passion
That which common death will devastate;
And may I never lift a pen, except to find
Where love lies hidden under every stone.

AT STEEP

i.m. Edward Thomas and Alun Lewis

I came to Steep on a summer's day and looked
Towards Selborne across the wooded, hilly land.
There Gilbert White had mused upon his swallows,
Autumn in and out had puzzled where they went . . .
But what I saw – the still air quick
With hunting wings, the earth more still
Unruffled by their sudden gust –
Was charged with what I knew,
A dream of peace more friendly to my eye
For being uttered by these dead . . .
And what I could not know,
Though preying shadows darkly stooped
Where now three generations met.

The one who came in honour of the first to die
Could not foresee a third to honour both,
Nor could the first have dreamt,
Until the end, a khaki shroud.
Each left this hillside, poet, naturalist and lover,
To find his arts could bend to skills of war;
That tramping after beauty in all weathers
Had supplied the stamina to march; discover
Habits of precision helped in learning drill
And detailed observation served another end
Than watching birds: who learned to kill.
And both were killed in less than thirty years;
And I had come at twenty-five, self-consciously
(Which they would understand), in reverence,
To stand at loss beneath the hawking birds
And look across the unchanged land; to make
In troubled prescience, a modest third.

LANDSCAPE

1 *Rock and Fern*

Inches away a beck slices the hill.
Catching my breath, I rest under the last thorn.
After it there's nothing green,
Only smooth stones, russet scrub,
And among the whin, rough stones.
But here, on a rock blanched by it,
The sun prints the shadow of a fern,
Still as a fossil, pointed like an arrowhead:
The mottoed tablet to an aeon.
A breeze jigs the fern,
And between moments of perfect white
The rock flickers. Then the wind stops
And the fern stiffens, a shadow bedded in rock.
Feeling invisible, I climb on.

2 *Rock and Water*

The beck strikes down,
Jabbing wittily through narrows,
Stopping to consider a slow pool
And sliding out cleanly over domes of rock.
At a bend the air decays,
Rotting for yards beyond the carcass,
Bone needles stuck through a mess of wool.

Bleached pates of rock, shreds of foam
Dull beside quartz, the sunstone glittering.
At intervals, unscoured rock piles
Keep a quiet like sacked monasteries.
And everything's hot to touch.
My shadow moons in a pool
Or lies crooked and breaking in shallows;
Delicately, a trout flicks through its head.

3 *At the Source*

Sheep jump up around me,
Their long skulls chock with horror.
The hills have heard little but bleating
Since the glaciers went by.

But I forget the pipit
Startled by my drudging boots, wrenching the eye
Upwards, the gaze beaten back
But for an instant free of spaces
Where a separate music's made.
I forget many things, mainly things:
The multiple unreckoned differences.
In the heat my hands swell and flush
Tightening the ring on my finger.

At the source
The mean bitten grass becomes mush
Reddish-brown, with islands of moss.
But I cannot call it the source.
The beck's been fed all the way
By others of equal size.
This one's no bigger than a puddle:
A small clear pool with a hint of iron.
I breathe over it, earthbound and aching.

The hills bleat.
The pipits address miles of air.

4 *A View from the Source*

The century drew out
Freighted with ore, jolting upline,
To stake with a bayonet acres of dead.

It had served; it could fail,
Poison the beck, and the beck
Empty its puffed white fish on the sea;
The place gutted, forgotten.

I can imagine the dark dispelled
By prosperous light; miners break earth;
All that's impossible
But ghosts in a place so dead.
A stone pitched in the shaft
Plummets from hearing with a metallic ring.

from **PEMBROKESHIRE JOURNEY**
for Peter Clarke

IV *Sleeping out on Pen Caer*

We are not mystics
Though this was their country:
Crested headlands
Like stone dragons drinking,

Haunt of hermit and guillemot;
Swirl of white islands
Where the current bore them,
Crucifix for pilot, among the seals.

We could have had a warm bed,
But chose discomfort, cold,
Feeling the earth
With our bones, under
The immense pale drifts of the Milky Way.

We have our whisky and tobacco.
We belong as much to jets
That pass above, as to the stars.

Before light the gulls' cries
Wake an older earth; hoarse and shrill,
The salt cry of rocky islands.

The sun appears, a red ball
Over the volcanic crags
Of Garn Fawr.

Out at sea the esses of a breeze
Lie like the marks of a lash
Flicked on a smooth insensible hide

TO THE UNKNOWN LABOURER

No monument
For time to smear;
No statue
That a man conceives
To trap himself in stone.

Only earth
Where a night's rain
Washed out his prints;
Chalk where his life
Was moulded;
Fields like hands after work,
Rough palms spread.

EASTER AT WHITE NOSE
i.m. Llewelyn Powys

Over downland, where the field
Of wheat in an arc
Drops into space,

We find the clean-cut lettered stone:

THE LIVING THE LIVING HE SHALL PRAISE THEE

The chalk is a globe bitten
Through its axis, the white line
Of retreating cliffs
Jagged with marks of teeth.
Far up in the salt wind,

Hearing the sea crumple
Mouthing its stones, I could lie
Here like ash if death only
Meant contemplation
Under the gently reddening

Sunlight and salt.
Old atheist, the new corn
Has forced a green way
Through flints to the edge
Of your stone. Like St Francis

You have stretched naked
On the naked ground, thankful
At Easter for the unholy
Resurrections, and sure
There was no other.

These flints teach the same
Dogma, and the brute wheat
Supports you with its fine green
Shoots; perhaps it is only
A wish almost as old to sense
That I speak to a mind
In the smooth domed hill.

NOBBUT DICK JEFFERIES

('See'd ye owt on the downs?'
'Nobbut Dick Jefferies moonin' about.')

No one but him
Mooning in a backwater
Of the nineteenth century

We've walked apart from the houses
And here, on the edge
Of a common under pines,
Light in every facet
Dances round his words

Such tenderness
Is unbearable:
The point of a grassblade
On the eyeball

Even from the flowerhead
Of a slender foxtail, a branch
Grows over the earth's side
And he has stopped where it bends
Trying the body's weight
Against the bough's strength

The knowledge
Will not disclose itself,
Nor the world make something
Of him, though the extremity
Starts from its roots.

AFTER PAUL NASH

1

With my own eyes:
A brilliant transfer
So far at the back of the head
Bone hardened round it,

Cross and swastika,
A stack of fallen devils
With astounded eyes.

Later, a dead sea,
The brain's root jarred
By metal waves.

2

Reversion of a distant field
On a chalky swell
To the primal amoeba.

With nests of skeletons
Under her skin, the nursing stone
Takes back the bomber
Of nineteen forty.

The sun communes with the sunflower,
The moon haunts the daylight
Like the artist's eye.

ELEGY FOR THE LABOURING POOR

1 *The Picturesque*

'There will soon be an end to the picturesque in the Kingdom.'
(John Constable, after the destruction, by fire, of Purns Mill.)

i

The picturesque is always with us.
Paint stiffens but the river swims forward;
Clouds move on and a mill becomes ash,
But the human features stay variable
And the pliant earth defies stasis.
And it is there, in that movement,
As another sky forms and a new generation
Measures the wood or levels the corn,
That the imagination commits itself
To an act that is elegy and salutation:
For what is welcomed – this continuity,
Is also change displacing the self that welcomes.
The carpenter alone commands a permanent living,
Elm perpetual usage. Nothing lasts
But the mortal nature of all that's unique.

ii

Near Bishopstone the family tended sheep
And ploughed the flint. There I glimpsed
A tractor fuming chalkdust
And found the fields worked profitably
But empty, smooth and pallid.
I came to the village under the downs
Whose graveyard held few stones –
The rest had ended in town cemeteries
Or been put to sea. Not one
Pushed a pen or was pushed by one.

Why grub in the past
For that life whose work seems fickle as ash?
Not to savour lachrymae rerum, nor toll
The general dirge that the globe goes round,
As the elegist wags a grave skull

Sonorous as a belfry: plough fossil,
Fossil pylon . . .
But to resurrect from the used land
The life that gave life; to utter it
As it cannot be known in the canvas
Where river and cloud stand fast,
Or in chronicles of the cold law;
As it can only be guessed by the self
Acknowledging change; as it can never be known.

2 *Forefather*

He moves like timber on a swell,
In mud gaiters and clay-coloured cord,
Bent to it, sculpting a furrow.
Mould's his name: James Mould
With shoots in Hants and Wiltshire.
His blunt boot-prints, fugitive
As the cloud at his rear,
Are unseen by the camera that exhumes
Celtic patterns from suave downland.
But the tread's purposeful.

His prayer's a bold harvest;
That the seed will stand up golden,
As an army, as mansions in Portland oolite,
As three loaves weekly.
God's ear is readier than Parliament's
Since He'll ferret in barn, byre and hen house,
Tithe hungry.
                    So he trudges,
Chained by daylight
To the round of a stiff field,
Deaf as yet to saucy agitation.
For living it is not, but a long starving.

3 'Gold Fever', 1830

After nightfall in harvest weather,
Over the lowland clay
Where the axe has opened hearts of oak,
A faint wind moves in the rigging of leaves.
On the quayside at Poole
Limestone waits shipment, and Portland
With its moon-grey scars butts into the sea.
Bored by the company of sheep
White horses gallop on the ridge of chalk,
But the Cerne giant, erect through an aeon,
Dreams of slackening into repose.
– Green man, fathering riches,
Delicate in the turn of a leafy wrist
Or puckish among moon-drunk sheaves,
Subject to none but the turning year,
Now fires in the labourer's veins,
Kindling the brand – and flexes strongly,
In the fist that will quench it,
Musket and shot and the outraged warrant
Of a mastering brain . . .

No man's lonelier than James Mould
As he wakes with stubble-scored legs
In a rat's refuge of wattle and daub.
At first the mist hangs clammy flags
But vanishes as the sun hardens
White-hot on flint, deadening the hedgerows.
Hunger isolates: however neighboured
In a common circumstance,
The body slogs alone, by rote,
And the jailed brain dulls
Fixed on the single motion – the arcing scythe
Deliberate as the sun at its habitual act.
Thus he swings through the day, a young man
Hard and spare as the grain

Now whispering in heaps,
Bent with his shoulder to the field,
Keeping it moving, glad of the work,
At a Klondyke near Bishopstone.

4 Captain Swing Fires the Workhouse

Rag bedding indelibly staled,
Lousy straw crusted with piss –
Tinder for the pyre.

Lit, the flames flick cleanly.
Like a candle in a turnip skull
The house makes a face in the dark.
The grass slithers with rats.
Then the windows stare out,
Splintering, and the fire explodes.
To a shepherd out on the downs
It's a cauldron fed by the oak,
As it ruins suddenly, lustily,
And the walls wither and the roof falls,
Pounding down timber and stone.
Like a yule log
It flickers on the watchful old.

Where's Swing?
The sergeant barks at his redcoats.
The magistrate chokes on latinate prose.

No one knows.
Not even a score of labourers
Cat-footing it through the underwood;
Among them, James Mould,
Daredevil as a boy again,
Pleased with himself and scared.

5 *The Voyage Out, 1831*

Bladder-wrack swaying in supple knots
Muddies the sunned quayside water.
Each for itself and each self
Viciously alike, the black-headed gulls
Snatch at refuse and their raw cries
Spread in circles, smacking the hulk,
Thinning out where the estuary opens
And the sea absorbs their voice.
But James Mould seeing the ocean
Sees only flint acres
Fought inch by inch, chalkdust rising,
And hears only his ghostly kin
Telling their names in the stunned brain.

When Portland pitches astern
And the last gull's torn shoreward,
Memory stays. The hulk bores on,
Shuddering, and the massive slabs break,
The clean fathomless wells slide open.
But the waves have faces
And the unbroken space narrows
To an inland patch of fields,
The chalk ridge, the sheep-walk scabious.

For this is purgation: to scour men
By divorcing them from all they know.
But the things they love go with them,
Untouchable, at times ferociously clear.
And what's left pleads after them,
And sours. Places are empty
That nothing but bitterness can fill.
The labourer voyages. The land uses
New methods, new men. But he takes with him
A life belonging to those acres
And leaves as a portion, the emptiness.

Under the downs, in countless sites
Gutted by the exile of their people,
Others will meet this isolation.
They will inherit the emptiness.

BIRTHDAY

When I wake, you are standing
Beside me. In the icy Victorian vase
Decorated with glass-cut fern,
You bring catkins, silver-grey

Pussy willow, and snowdrops.
A fine yellow powders your hand.
It is late March, the cold earth
Is broken and out of darkness

You bear a gift. I marvel, love,
To have been born for this.

THERE

As sett to badger dark in the warm soil;
As moist places to the secret mole;
As essential darkness to earth itself:
Love, the night surrounds us.
We are the confluence of underground streams.
We grow together and in daylight
Flow out apart, now each in each, remade.

EARTH POEMS

1 *Song of the Earth*

Bring or do not bring your mind's distress.
The seas it foundered in
Are none of mine.

My words are flint, cold to your touch.
They tell I am
What you become.

No tree bore the branch
From which your sick thoughts spin.
There is no vertigo in falling leaves.

Along brain's empty dancing-floor
My small blades creep.
The grass's flood-tide bears you home.

2 *At the Edge*

You will haunt the edges
Becoming more shadowy the more
This world streams past.
Now there is nothing but grassblade
Running into grassblade,
Each a separate wave where the colours flux
Orange into brown. The field is going out
With the autumn tide,
And where you were there is now
Only a cry.

3 *The Elements*

Even a poor eye
Can see clear through the globe

To its Antipodes. All, all,
Like a frail door banging in the wind,
A leaky raft through which the sea springs,
Cannot keep out the other elements.
With faculties so weak
You can reach out to touch the other side of death.

LANDSCAPE OF THE DAYLIGHT MOON

I first saw it inland.
Suddenly, round white sides
Rose through the thin grass
And for an instant, in the heat,
It was dazzling; but afterwards
I thought mainly of darkness,
Imagining the relics of an original
Sea under the chalk, with fishes
Beneath the fields. Later,
Everywhere upon its surface
I saw the life of the dead;
Circle within circle of earthen
Shells, and in retraced curves
Like finger marks in pale sand,
The print of a primaeval lover.
Once, climbing a dusty track,
I found a sunshaped urchin,
With the sun's rays, white
With the dusts of the moon.
Fetish, flesh become stone,
I keep it near me. It is
A mouth on darkness, the one
Inexhaustible source of re-creation.

LANDSCAPE OF THE WINTER SUN

The sun, over the ridge,
Refines its stony bulk
To an airy whiteness.
Light glancing draws the eyes
Upwards, to the centre;
But a glimpse closes them.
When sight clears, there are
Fiery points in irregular patterns
Across the field; in intricate
Bare hedges blackthorn leaves
Edged with ice; distances
Where, in a few months,
None will exist. For a time
It is as if the sun looks
At a landscape it has
Simplified, until, standing
On a bank for the view,
I am surprised by a shadow's
Comical stick-like elongation
Spanning a small field.

I was with the first inhabitant
In these hills and I stayed here
After him, at the foot of his grave

MATRIX

A memorial of its origins, chalk in barns and churches
moulders in rain and damp; petrified creatures swim in
its depths.

　　It is domestic, with the homeliness of an ancient
hearth exposed to the weather, pale with the ash of
countless primeval fires. Here the plough grates on an
urnfield, the green plover stands with crest erect on a
royal mound.

　　Chalk is the moon's stone; the skeleton is native to its
soil. It looks anaemic, but has submerged the type-sites
of successive cultures. Stone, bronze, iron: all are assimi-
lated to its nature; and the hill-forts follow its curves.

　　These, surely, are the work of giants: temples
re-dedicated to the sky god, spires fashioned for the
lords of bowmen:

　　Spoils of the worn idol, squat Venus of the mines.

　　Druids leave their shops at the midsummer solstice;
neophytes tread an antic measure to the antlered god.
Men who trespass are soon absorbed, horns laid beside
them in the ground. The burnt-out tank waits beside
the barrow.

　　The god is a graffito carved on the belly of the chalk,
his savage gesture subdued by the stuff of his creation.
He is taken up like a gaunt white doll by the round hills,
wrapped around by the long pale hair of the fields.

FOUND OBJECTS

1

A reindeer bone carved
in the reindeer's likeness.
Saddle-quern
Loom-weight
Spindle-whorl.
A chalk phallus.
A lump of chalk
with heavy curves bearing
the image of woman.

2

A necklace with blue beads
of Egyptian faience, black ones
of Kimmeridge shale.
Slingstone
Cannon ball
Cartridge.
A phallus carved on the church wall.
A statuette of the Virgin.

3

A coin worn headless,
with a disarticulate horse.
Cartwheel
Crank-shaft
Flash-bulb.
A bust of the death-god
cast in imperishable alloy.

FOSSIL URCHINS

A tribe found them, believing
They grew like dandelions
In the soil.
                An exquisite
From the Age of Fishes
Became the sun's icon,
                        crowned with rays,
And a ring of suns,
Sacred to the resurrection,
Was placed around the dead.

There is still
A touch of man.
They are composed
Of blood and fire,
Where the sun roots in the earth.
They are not clammy like potsherds,
But shapely, and warm to the hand.

FLINTS

They are ploughed out,
Or surface under surface

Washes away leaving the bleached
Floor of a sunken battleground.

Some are blue with the texture of resin,
The trap of a primeval shadow.

Others are green,
A relic of their origins.

The white one is
An eye closed on the fossil.

Worked in radial grooves
From the bulb of percussion

They shed brittle flakes.
The core with its brutal edge

Shaped the hand.

THE AGE OF MEMORY

It is over three hundred years since the churchwarden
paid a carpenter three and tenpence for converting the
maypole into a town ladder.

The puritan is a good toolmaker. He contracts his
workforce from the boozy remnant whooping in the ring.

Even a backwater is shaken by purposeful tremors,
when it empties. Afterwards, the place is greener. The
native god is exposed for the first time.

If the god is a spectacle, he is no longer blind. In the
scheme of things he becomes guardian of the dead. He is
invested with memory. The insignia of office is an
invisible globe.

TOTEM

Where are the giant's people?
They have followed the mole
Under mounds. The Dance
Is a ring of stones.

48

Soon there will be nothing
But a breeze gathering dust
Over pale fields, a maze
Of ditches scored on the hill,

Unless a man stand naked
Of all but imagination.
Let him discover me.

I rise through him
Or lie here and wait,
Scratched in the chalk.

THE GIANT'S BOAST

I was before Christ, and I remember
The saurian head of my begetter.
I conceived these words at my creation,
When you traced your shadow on the stone.

I was before Moses, and his fury
Returned me to the elements,
From which I am remade.

I have walked with my ribcage naked,
When the strong man dug his grave.
I have contemplated the skeleton
Under the flesh of all things,
And I gave to the holy waters
A natural potency.

The smoke from a wicker basket
Was sweetest to my nose;
For I have levelled and engendered
Multitudes, and I do not answer
To a single name.

No man understood me
Who called me brutal, and no woman
Who called me kind.
Mothers and daughters worshipped me.
I worshipped with my body
The naked ground.

THE GIANT'S SHADOW

I am the giant who carries a giant
On his back.
This is my comrade.
Is he alive or dead?

I stoop and cry out,
Let go, let go.
When I look up
The shadow hangs over me
With crossed wings . . .
Impure fancies, how they breed
In the sludge
Of a standing mind!

Do you imagine the dead stop in their graves?
Stones of the abbey that vanished
Are mounted on my spine.
This is history,
When the mind is an open grave.

You are sunlight,
You are darkness,
Green god.
The rest is illusion.
Illusion with talons hooked through my bones.
It is an anchor
From the bottom of the sea,

It is fixed in the floor of the sea
Like an ax-head fast in a skull.
If I could move it, the world would shift.

How heavy the shadows are!
I wrestle with them all day long,
Finger clutched round my cold stave.

EARTH-BORNE

Though they called my people
Dwellers by the water,
I am no sailor, least of all
A Celtic saint.

Far from the sea, too far,
I am nostalgic for their lives,
For the green sea of darkness
And beaked wave.

Where the wind and tide quarry,
And in an instant smash,
The green-veined slabs of stone,
They give the tiller to the tide,
As if provided for.

No sons of Aphrodite, shell-borne
Zealots gaunt as your stone cross,
The wandering limpet knows its home.
I am too much your opposite:
Earthbound, as if the earth
Were not a sea.
My fingers, bloodless, white,
Are knotted to a stick I cannot drop.

THE GIANT'S CLUB

It was here from the first,
An oak branch,
Shaped like a leaf,
Growing from my hand.

I am a man
Carved from an oak
Traced on a stone
Cut in the chalk.

Why do you lie to me,
Setting giant
Against giant,
One savage, with the club
Of annihilation,
Which the other evades?

It is I, whom you call
Priapus, who bear the club.

If it rots,
It is not a limb
To amputate.
Without it, I fall.

Phallus and club are one ground.
Terror is their separation
In the mind; the other face
Of terror, your indulgent smile.

WHAT IS A GIANT MADE OF?

I have seen myself
Standing defiantly
Apart from the hill,
And I have seen,
Through earth's tissue
And a sky
Without foundation,
The daylight moon,
Brittle as a chalk fragment,
Reflecting my disdain.

What is a giant made of?

There is a clump
Of flowering blackthorn
Spattered with the dung
Of rooks: these, too,
Are the giant,
These white flecks.
There my eye sleeps
With its mirrors turned
To the wall of my skull,
And beneath me
I feel the grass rise
And fall, like the slow
Deep breaths of a giantess.

A CHALK PEBBLE

This is perfect:
A chalk pebble,
Smooth and round,
Like an egg
With the foetus

Of a giant
Curled inside.

When I touch it,
My hand crumbles.
The hill is a fine cloud
Whitening the Cretaceous sea.

Starfish, urchin, sponge,
I have become many:
We do not trespass here,
Composed on the white floor.
We are not foreign to this ground.

Who is the saurian
Tyrannizing the shallows,
Smashing a trackway
Through the new green trees?
His familiar,
Disproportionate head
Is small and mean.

The giant turtle is in its element,
Housed on the summit
Of low white hills.
The dead sponge mingles
With alchemic water
For the slow formation
Of a perfect stone.

CHALK MOON

How it leeches the mind,
When a daylight moon rises
Like a piece of the hills.

There is no darkness here;
The living are so remote.
Even the club feels powdery,
Crushed in my hand.

The sea has withdrawn far out;
Streams cannot reach it.
They die of thirst
In a landscape picked to the bone.

When the wind blows
My breath tastes of dust.

ONE FLESH

I raise my arm
And the club's chalk stem
Branches from my hand.

I kick out my legs
And the phallus extends
Like a belemnite.

I force a passage
In the shape of my body
From the chalk,

And emerge offensively,
Brandishing weapons,
About to shake off the dust.

THOSE WHO HAVE NOTHING

They still seek me,
Those who have nothing.
Others consume their plenty
And look away.

They watch as the night grows colder.
They breathe on the clenched hill.

I take from them
A little warmth
And carry under my ribs
The impression of bodies
Formed in the dew.

THE PROTECTOR

I was made naked
To protect men
From evil spirits.

I was given the club
To protect them
From the tangible.

When the ghouls whicker
Around my nakedness,
Exchanging sex and club,
I become their reflection
And they rot.

DAWN

There is a moment
No one sees,
When earth is formed
In the image of neither
Mist nor light.

Grey flowers grow
On the giantless hill,
Over the untouched graves.
Sleeper and sleepless lie
Without a name.

Colour breaks and this day
Is one of the millions,
Bloodred, gold, with a streak
Of unearthly green
Like the eye of a god.

Dawn is perfection
Of a kind. Now I wake
To the unfinished act
And the dead lie complete
For ever, under their names.

THE MOTHERS

I know this land; it was made
In the image of the Mothers.
Even now it makes me sick,
Living on a roller that never breaks.

It is white under the plough, and so smooth
The eye cannot stand.
It is always winter here
And the moon looks down, pleased.

I was made to stand against this,
A rude bulwark the grass ignores.
Every man is a defiant boy
Defiling the tits of a giantess.
He is drowned many times over
In his own seed.

Man's image of a man:
Stone Age and omnipotent,
Subduing with two weapons:
After brutality, tenderness . . .

Even the chalk is female.
It has not stopped laughing
For two thousand years.

DEVIL

Who was the goat upon hindlegs
Who tickled with a whiskery thigh
The hairless monk?

When the young friar drowsed
I drew with his goosequill in the margin
Pictures of beasts and birds.

He saw a devil to castrate,
Initialled in God's name between my legs,
Jehovah Destroyed This.

Though weather rubbed it out,
This was God's patent for the age.

I am the pupil of the eye,
Diminished by a cool, bored look.

MOTHER AND CHILD

One in the earth
Crouches, a skeleton
With a skeleton
In her arms.

The other
On the tower
Chills me with her purity,
Draws me to her warmth.

I listen to the silence,
Leaning down
From the crumbling arms
Of the hill.

ABORIGINE

Streams dig with their flints.
Chalk rises through stubble
Like a moon. From this page
I learnt my name.

Everything refers me back
In time. Chalk words. Flint words.
The chalk are porous, and crumble.
The flint are hard.

I am bound to the place
By its language.
I was taught to speak
In such metaphors.

When I am dead the language
Will shed me. Till then
It takes something of me
Wherever it goes.

THE GIANT'S FORM

What does the child scrawl
On the smooth flat top
Of a tomb?

Augustine's well,
With cold green lights,
May spring through flint.
Here, within
The burial ground,
He thrust his staff
Into the earth:
                    I see God!

Now let the saint
Give back his halo
To the sun, and to the earth,
Adopted sanctity;
For should the grass
Grow through my sides,
The playing fingers
Of a child

Would still depict,
With blind recall
On some flat stone,
The giant's form.

YELLOWING MOON

The rotted flints alone
Are motionless. They lie
In half-light, blue scars
Touching, under the barley.

Hardly a patch shows white.
Shadow softens the glare
Of tracks. These are nights
Of the yellowing moon.

Now fire-tints melt
Enclosures, run fields together
In one broad curve
Of ripening grain.

A pigeon flaps away;
Heat-haze resolves it
In a dozen yards
Into a burr of energy.

Nothing is self-contained.
There is no standing apart,
Of tree, or barn, or man.
I am possessed like a single stalk.

THE SIREN

Death, too, is a profession.
It has its orders and degrees.
The finality
Of an inscription
Exalts the hand.

Tympany of the Nordic storm-god,
Basso profundo, tumid with doom.

On a pipe made from swan's bone
The siren always plays
Her softer airs.

ELEGY FOR THE GIANTS

Scorn broke them; they softened,
Mouldering like touchwood.
An effigy found in an attic,
Lugged out to be burnt,
Was once the molten god.

Beggared Herakles became a clown
And as the clodpole with a stave,
Beelzebub, invited blows
And laughter. They bragged
And bluffed and roared,
Jaws gored with rouge,
Exalting some boy-hero
By their fall.
Like Ysbadaddan,
All were well shaved.

Others turned to stone.
They wear grey habits
With an austere dignity.
They are upright, with ascetic faces.
They have fallen and do not plead.

MOCKERY

Though delight fails me and the will dies,
I am the involuntary prodigal.
As always I sign myself
Your obedient servant
And because all things bear it
My name breeds contempt.

Here the migrant renews its cycle,
Here the young goat shivers
And foliage greens the naked horn,
Here the old track starts from the source,
From here it is never the same.
It is through me, always.

I laugh at conceptions of genius.
With mockery the fool announces his birth.

THE SPRING

Let there be peace between us,
Tortured god.
Like a lesser sun,
The light of your church
Once cast my shadow.
I sprouted horns
Like a Lord of Beasts.

I am no longer strong
In my strength;
And you, no longer strong
In your weakness,
Can you accept this water,
Once sacred to me,
That your blessing cursed?

BEFORE THE SCOURING

It begins under the skin
As a prickle.
Grass blades
Work through the ribs.
Sight blurs to a tangle of hair.
I begin to merge with the hill.

Heat cracks the skin;
Frost flakes it;
Wind disperses the dust
And what it leaves
Rain washes down.
I begin to merge with the air.

Every few centuries
Something is lost.
A lion skin. The navel.
Perhaps a name.

AFTER THE SCOURING

It is almost a re-creation:
The same bludgeon,
The same phallus,
The aboriginal stare.

I'm stiff with the lust
Of centuries.
I'm white with rage.

I'll tear myself out of the hill
And leave it in pieces.

A little loose chalk stirs an inch.
Seeds tickle my ribs.
Nothing else moves.

Seven years will be soon enough
To try again.

NOVELTY

You call me old,
But to the wind I am
A novelty, and to the rain
No more than the shallows

Of a man-shaped stream.
As for the earth, I barely
Exist. It is early yet
To speak of extinction,

Though we each keep
A different time. If,
To survive, I am less than
Human, my image forms

Between you and the ground.
Alone, I cut a feeble figure.
Only admit we belong
To each other, and begin.

STASIS

I strain to reach downwards
Out of the glare.
I am closed out.
Dust seals my mouth.

Nothing moves
But a glittering point
Scratching a chalk track
Across the sky.

Every surface reflects
My lifted arm.
If I could move
I would destroy them.

Failure does not teach me patience.
When I am exhausted,
There is a gust of darkness,
A smell of water on the air.

SOLSTICE

Is the poppy afraid
Of its redness?
I am not a dry leaf
That flares to nothing.

Roots drink at my side.
Chalk absorbs my warmth.
And still I am replete,
Blood-ripe.

The facets of every flint
Glow red. No surface
Remains unkindled
To reflect my stare.

All day sun passes
Through me.
I am burned on the hillside
With its brand.

PRAYER IN WINTER

Give me courage, hunter,
When energy has bled down
To the roots and the moon
Is a chalk pebble hurled
Into the sky, when rain
Turns dust to sludge
And the wind hacks my groin.

Give me the courage
Of your slow retreat
From the frozen springs, following
The signs of reindeer and bison.
When life retreats, let me
Follow the signs.

HEIL

Heil, they shout. *Heil*.

Wolves are my kinsmen.
Beneath each wolfskin,
A guttural peasant.

Heil, Heil.

They deafen the oracle
With their shouting.

Heil, Heil.

How shall I defeat the darkness
I am part of?
The hero gores himself
Wrestling the dragon.

THE GIANT'S NAME

In which district the god Helith was once worshipped.

Here, in darkness, come the humble members of Christ's
body. *In quo pagim* the risen Christ gleams; but Helith
smoulders, reddened by the peasant's breath.

Our high admiral Hercules.

This is the ship of England, carved from a single oak. Her
master is navigant of the obscure passage, a hard-headed
merchant with a fabulous map. He descends into the pit,
and wrestles with the furnace. His labours are wrought
in iron.

Helith; that is holy stone – or a corruption of Helios,
the sun? A sunstone, pediment in earth. The ground is
dense with holy names: Elwood, Elston Hill, Elwell,
Yelcombe (*y el cwm*). Was there a standing stone on
Elston Hill before Helith was fleshed out below the
Trendle? *Where beth they, beforen us weren?*
Make your enquiry of the dust.

I make no enquiry there. Give me a living name.

A WIND OFF THE SEA

It exhausts me at last,
This querulous petition
Of a chalk Hamlet
To the ground.

The sea-wind needs
No addition from complaints;
It has touched
Chert and flint,

Left the smooth boulder
Unmoved, but acquired
Something of the character
Of stone. I leave

My mouth as its portion.
Let it resolve my breath
Into a taste of salt,
A scent of thyme,

A touch of stone.
My image I leave
To whoever it reflects;
But my body is the sea's;

It is a piece broken
From the hill, a chalk
Stack, not formed,
But worn down by the tides.

from
SOLENT SHORE
1978

1 FORESHORE

NEW YEAR'S DAY AT LEPE

Set out on a morning of white thaw
smoking between oaks, Hatchet Pond so still
it might have been frozen
except for the long slender rods
as if painted on its dark blue glaze.
Saw nothing of the *Private, Keep Out*
notices of semi-feudal estates,
but cock pheasants in brown fields
of sharp-edged clods, poking out their necks.
Then the small rusty bell of the shingle
tinkled and grated as it dragged,
a shadowy tanker bared its round stern
and Marchwood power station exhaled
a breath which the sun tinged pink;
but of all things none seemed newer
than gravel with its sheen of fresh oranges
at the water's lip. Brought away that,
and an old transparent moon
over the Island, the delicate industrial sky
blue-grey as a herring gull's back,
and a small sunny boy running beside
the great wet novelty shouting *wasser, wasser.*

PAINTINGS
for my father

Avon weir pouring

suspended, the race
brushed still, river
and sky, shadow,
sunlight and trees rushing

enclosed, opening
the house on water.

Slow Boldre,
slower Stour:
gold shallows;
dark, Forest pools

or where they run
dammed – white whorl
of an eddy, or flow
barred – green, brown

pass from seclusion
of leaf and earth,
blue oils spreading
contained:

Christchurch fluid
on the wall,
the shore at Keyhaven
where an easel stood.

BIRTHPLACE

Nights begin underground.

In the morning
wine cellars stand
flung open
in the medieval town,

and below basements, below
floors of chipped flint,
the gravels and clay sink down.

Helmets come bobbing in.

Waving a piece of weed
I run along the shore.

SHINGLE-SPIT

Where the next moment
wiped out the last impression
the sea had raised
a wall of shingle.
Slippery reefs of kelp
blotched the water; sandbars
barely covered, shone like bullion.
The Island showed plainly
what it was: the splintered foot
of a bridge, and on a surface
hacked into crests
the chalk blue waves reflected it.
They broke, of course,
and a slow, dark pulse
beat rhythmically in the sand.
It will not be like that now,

and was not then.
I expected to hold nothing visible,
and did not, though my steps
remade a pattern they had long become.

RAT ISLAND

1
With first light
The bearings surface.

From Tennyson's memorial
To Sway tower,
From Jack in the basket
To Fawley,
Point after point
Rises on time.

I mark them,
Borne back
On a freshening wind.

The sea completes the circle.

2
There are no rats;
Except at high spring,
No island.

Only a relic
Of the late defences
Harbouring
Mud-dwellers.

Part of the shore
That curves away,
Keen as a tern's wing.

3
I have stayed long enough
Casting a shadow.

Let it be
As it is
When a tern dives
And on the blue sky
In the water, between
The smooth hulls
Of mudbanks,
The wind casts waving lines.

PITTS DEEP

Over Abbey ploughland
On a brown, winter day
Of Cistercian calm,
No one will go observing
The silver bell mouth of the sky,
Or cross the manorial path
Into oakwoods descending
Almost to the water –
Except, perhaps, two friends
With a bottle of cheap wine
Who walk in confessional mood
Where forest ponies also go,
Trampling soiled, silky weed
On mudbanks and quills
Of bleached salt-grass,
Sowing a trail of droppings
On the stilled shore.

FRIEND WITH A MANDOLIN
for Jim Insole

Singer with a mandolin,
Pluck from the smoke
Of a humdrum bar
The raw defiant strings
Of Mountjoy and Van Diemen's Land,

Let the bland south
Hear the blues.

From the cradle
Twanging in your hands,
Pick Café Mozart.

At closing time, we'll sit out
On the shingle drunkenly
Amazed to think of France,
So far away, still serving wine.

UNDER HORDLE CLIFFS

Where I go crab-wise
Gardens have fallen, and houses
On the rusty cliffs follow,
Blankly returning the look of the sea.

Here the beach turns, bedding
A white trunk.

Above all the Island rises,
Like shattered bone;
In blue, watery light
More cloud than skull . . .

Is the sea also
Drunk with repetition,
Hearing under all sounds
The name it cannot speak?

It has rolled
Shingle waves after us,
Over and over,
Forming new hollows.

In places covered
Or unmade, under flints
Crusted with salt,
The smothered fire burns.

WEST WIGHT

Was it idolatry or love?

Nettles hide the sign.
Through the heart
of this deep green hollow
the road leads on.

Then on the high domed crown
thyme and all grass end
gulls shriek below
nothing to lean on but the wind.

Do not ask me to take you there,
no, not for a phial of coloured sand.

Stand with me here on the shore,
watching the white island,
stark as a statue, fall into mist.

Turn back with me, always
turn back, my love.

BY SOUTHAMPTON WATER

The water is bottle green, with a salt crust
And an unmistakable flavour of sewage.

A tarred gull floats past; an orange box
And the helmet of a marine; a glove
With the hand still in it.

Going home,
The view from Totton flyover
Makes me gape
Even now.
                    The river's wedge broadens
Seaward; a dream of cranes swims in haze;
Smoke from the power station silvers the blue.
Everywhere, men I know work under it.
Necessities are unladen and shipped.
That is the root.

Black ribs of a hull in the mud.
'It's a Viking,' my parents said.

'Viking': the word's a skeleton of spars
With sky through it,
Sticking up from blue-grey mud.

As the song goes:

>   *When the tide is out at Totton*
>   *The stench is something rotten* . . .

True; but I cannot imagine sea without it;
Without gumboot-sucking ooze;
Small green crabs sidling by old green posts;
Without tugs and the giant Queens.

At night, crossing to Hythe,
The water squirms with ideograms.

I could spare a life trying to decipher them.

THE WATER'S EDGE

In a time between
flying boat and hovercraft,
between stained tanks
through villages, and waves
of Solent City:

in a place over
caved-in paths echoing
the tidal swill,
over windrows of shell
and beaker: here

I return, like sun
on the river's green back
that cannot pierce it,
or remain, like stones
I once threw, working
a blind passage in the mud.

Though waves set hard
along the coast,
and new amphibians
displace the old,
part of me stays
at the water's edge,
greased with use, among
corks, tarred feathers,
bits of boats, tins
knocking against the wall.

SOLENT WINTER

1

Yachts on the leaden estuaries
are wingless, larval.
Leeward of the island
rusty bums of tankers
squat in the swell.
This full-bodied water
bears its trademark in oil.

Now the tides grease a shore
stripped to its working parts.
High over the cranes
Fawley Beacon burns.

2

On short dim evenings
the grey island floats off-shore
like a ghostly berg;
liners are lit up for Christmas
with the stores.

Where Southampton Water forks
the town is grounded
on gravel shoals.
Funnels converge on the centre.
Portholes and windows shine.
The streets trap echoes
of muted horns.

Wires still buzz with messages
from the *Titanic*.
A séance breaks up
when a cabin-boy screams.

ON A PHOTOGRAPH OF SOUTHAMPTON DOCKS
for Brian Maidment

Blinding silver on grey,
a suntrack points deep
into this average morning.
All is ready for work:
launches at their moorings,
small tubs off the pierhead,
warehouses; and above all
the cranes, these flying high
or with pulleys dangling,
those far back, more spidery.
No, it is not their function
to please the eye.
Yet they do – more so
for the common goodness
of their function, for grace
extra to a working world
that neighbours sky and water,
drawing from all
some ordinary tribute;
for that reason too,
more beautiful, as they say:
like birds, like dancers.

HOLY ROOD

Below Bar, through the gate
That is always open,
Many made the passage
Grief makes back.

Only the great anchor
In the bombed church
Will not drag.

Its fluke in the nave
Holds all who pass
To brief observance,

But leaves a centre
That is always fixed
Where all stream through.

CANUTE ROAD

'Go back,' he says,
knowing it won't,
the long tide standing.
Yet it does, over and over again,
greening gravel with weed,
and leaving now and then
a hand-axe or faceless coin.
Image passes into image,
name under name, down the road
between medieval gatehouse
and docks, that ends with a cold smell
where the floating bridge runs out
and shipyards dominate the shore.

FLOATING-BRIDGE

You look for
a good haul
in green, milky water
where chains slide over reels.

Is it, perhaps, the sludge
of nostalgia, or the unseen
seen too narrowly?

Whatever it is,
the chains go deep.

FROM A PILL-BOX ON THE SOLENT

On a day of ripped cloud,
Angled light, wind against tide,
I am tempted to begin
The story of my life.

Waves come from far off,
Through the gap they have made,
Between Purbeck and Wight.

Surf booms in the pill-box,
Rattles the shingle,
Folds over it, unfolds,
Laying it bare.

Let it blow sand or salt.
Here at least I tread without fear
Of unsettling dust.

SOLENT SHORE

Where the shoreline ends
At the horizon, the far sky's
Pronged with orange flames
From the refinery.

Today the clouds bear east,
Forming a broad, shadowy space
Of dark green mudlands,
Staked out with old stumps,
With rows of masts along
Estuaries and creeks.

It might be almost any time,
As one slow hulk of cloud
Lags to the west, mirrored
Like an oil slick off the Needles.

RICE GRASS
(Spartina Townsendii)

Praise one appearing
lowly, no man's rose,
but with roots far-reaching
out and down.

Give homage to a spartan cross,
native and American,
hardier and more adaptable
than those; nearly a newcomer
but one that, by staying put
has made itself a home;
also a traveller east and west.

Celebrate the entertainer
of sea aster, sea lavender,
thrift and nesting gulls;
lover of mud and salt;
commoner and useful colonist,
converter from ooze
of land where a foot may fall.

MARY ROSE (1545)

Sunk by her own guns
cannoning to leeward,
gunports open to the sea.

The King he screeched
like any maid:
'Oh my gentlemen.
Oh my gallent men.'

All over. The cry of mun,
the screech of mun, Oh Sir,
up to the very heavens.

The very last souls I seen
was that man's father
and that man's.

Drowned like rattens,
drowned like rattens.

WITNESSES

1
In a manner dying
  with age, but –

Tide's coming up!
  bears wine
cleare & white hued,
faire orient red.

Not always must a man
close his eyes
clench his teeth
filter the stuff
wry mouthed & shuddering.

Not at Clausentum
for patrons of Ancasta.

Not at Suthamtun.

Or over undercrofts
built on tuns of wine,
woolsacks, woolfells.
  Agnus Dei.

No other men than
gilded merchants,
no other world but England.

2

Tide's coming up!
  bears ever
a floating population,
carrack & galley, wherry & cog.

Long oarsmen
of Hamwic, Wulfheard's kin,
graves dug through graves
under the gasworks.

Confluent founders,
incendiaries: Francons;
Fleming burgesses;
Latin tenders
  of goods and names.

Dalmatian oarsmen,
patrons of St Nicholas,
sharing a grave.

Men of Northam
boasting of Alfred.
Men of Itchen
boasting of Olaf.

  Floating,
  ever-rolling,

their oars drip silver.

3
It's a long haul
from the Watergate, or Bargate.
For Cambridge, Gray and Scrope
the wind sets foul.

 A long haul
for the poor naked foot.
For musters; regiments
with limbers, horses, mules.
For men and women
 of Area C.

 Undercrofts
shelter them, or they trudge
with prams and pushcarts;
wander the woods
 till morning.

Between booms,
after epidemics,
 in a manner dying.

Not always must a man
doctoring the poor
die of his vocation.

All the same for them.
Where can we go?
 We have complained
till we are tired.

 Dying
over curative waters;
docks from mudlands;
arrivals, departures.

Enduring
our continual stream
to the land of gold.

2 *EBB*

TIDE-RACE

High water: the sea asleep
In oily ripples, rocking
A bleared, whole sun.
Then the tide begins to turn,
Gathering speed, bores
Tunnels through wrack,
Ploughs deep furrows
Through a shingle blizzard.
Where bass may keep their heads
A six-ounce lead trips away,
Dancing over ledges; the fisherman,
Woken by a shrieking ratchet,
Is hooked for an instant fast
In the running sea, before
His line flies loose. Drumming
Under his feet, cresting where
It brushes a shoal, shouldering
The adjacent slack into ridges,
The broad channel races through,
White sparks flying from its back.

WHERE THE GRAVEL SHELVES

From the shallows of sleep,
Out where the gravel shelves,
The sharp white rocks passing,

The shore, the open sea, passing,
Taller the white rocks,
Farther the shore, closer
But less attainable
The open sea . . .
You, chin above water,
Always afraid of the undertow,
The firm foot slipping, you
Whose strongest emotion was fear
Approach now the dreamless, deep
Stillness, silent as a ship's bell
Stopped with a bell of mud.

GRACEDIEU (1418–)

No ungodly siege,
no maiden voyage.

Her unwritten log
a stroke of lightning,
decay near the key

from which she sailed
upstream,
to a mud berth.

Her good timber made
roofs shipshape.
Her rotten beams breed
untrue histories.

Ghost of a Viking.

Shadowy virgin
gracing the silt.

PROSPECT OF BOLDRE CHURCH

Raised above oaks
Above a full river.

Once the living
Of William Gilpin.
Now his quiet mansion.

He hopes to rise
In God's good time.

Dim, coloured light
Stains the sanctuary,
The lettered stones
Charged with patience.

Things that seem misplaced
Catch the eye
Irresistably,
Even as it bends:

H.M.S. Hood;
The Book of Remembrance,
Names illuminated
Of the able-bodied.

The head inclined to bow
Remains unshocked,
But cold; observes

St Nicholas
Overlooking benches
Carved with her crest;
Pictures the sea

Outside the frame: colder
For fires quenched in a flash,
For steel made a harrow
Useless on the ocean bed;

Even here, enclosed
Above oaks above
A full river, the sea
Open, spirited shipless.

AT OSBORNE HOUSE

Under cedar and ilex,
On lawns to us *verboten,*
Convalescents watch us,
From coach and car,
Mobbing their repose.

         His too,
Albert of Saxe-Coburg's,
His bay of Naples, his
Renaissance villa,
His evergreens, which,
After more than a century,
Cast longer and darker shadows.

If it were quiet, if
I could attend,
I might imagine
Innumerable salutes,
         the waterway
Busy with despatches,
Screwed and churning,
Hatched with white, cross lines.

Among her many possessions
The Empress of grief
Becomes her statue,
                    marble
Among marble and horn,
Silver and ivory, mahogany and teak.

Here is India, here
St Petersburg
On a vase of Nicholas I,
Here Kaiser Wilhelm
Of the waxed aspiring moustache.
                              The musical-box
Plays a march from *Tannhauser.*

She is Britannia;
To her Neptune entrusts
The Command of the Sea.

The finish is perfect,
A spectacle,
Complete –
Like the royal children's marble limbs.

I would rather look out,
Down terraces of statuary,
Over woods of oak and beech,
Elms dying or dead,
To the blue Solent,
Spithead,
The tower blocks of Portsmouth.

The young Queen bathing
For the first time
Ducked her head:
'I thought I should be stifled.'

On the balcony with Albert
She heard the nightingales.
Here, by royal decree
The past tense shall prevail.

AT THE STATUE OF ISAAC WATTS

1
Image set
Among sticky buds:

Dated, the marble
Establishes a prodigal
Home for good.

Clear through traffic,
Trains and horns
The Civic Centre chimes
'O God, our help . . .'

2
The measured tide
Moves congregations;
Its undertow sways
Outside the walls.

Across the narrow sea
From Western Shore
(Refinery hazy
Under the Forest)
An impure land delights.

Against sluggard wit
And muddy spirit,
Dr Watts stands proof.

At his granite base,
Place tributary strands
Of living wrack.

SLACK

All along wave crests
Catch sunlight,

For an instant roll
Over smooth; then stream
Up the beach a fetch
Of tumbling pebbles
And wash of sandy foam.

Waves after wave run in,
But each breaks perceptibly
Shorter than the last.

The shore dries towards them,
Yellow advances on grey.

Ebb falls slack.

Again the body waiting
Has felt mouth burn dry,
Hard light flood the shell.

Has held fast still,
Though moonshine
Made dark translucent,
And the wild bed of wrack

And stones a water-meadow
Not embittered by tides.

Held fast, and again
By filaments of sense,

Wanting, not wanting,
The sea advancing back.

OTHER

Breakers and wind
Are blinding,
And drown the voice.

Likewise a calm and open sea
Sucks up, casts back,
All images – or else

They are suddenly distant,
Tiny figures just seen, gone
Where the beach curves.

The artist steps through his canvas.

The vociferous I alone
Who made the head ache
With his clapper,
Is an empty bell;

A cave where wind echoes
And dark tongues absorb
The metallic light.

Now the gull's shrilling
Above the wind, or quiet *huk-huk*,
Is a note among many
Belonging to one, one
That is not a voice;

Nor meaningless, unless
Extrinsic meanings
Are found: patterns the wind
Does not draw, webs
Between waves the foam
Does not make.

POSTSCRIPT
in memory of Vivienne

Alive, no
doubt of that, no
doubt when shingle
kicks my ankle bone

And lightning splits
my clouded mind

A Baez song:
sweet voice through
fall of hair
                    black hair
                    long fingers
picking a guitar
                    long fingers
picked

And lightning –
                daggers
twisted   scattered
silver points

A tall lithe figure
                races
up the shelving spit
between the mud-banked estuary
& sea

I lag behind
                Or
Floating pools
on pools,
a mirage
icy blue, dark blue

Stopped wordless
till the stones grew cold
when hand in hand . . .

Those letters now
(if kept)
are monologues
                were
monologues

(You said
I never saw you
'As I am')

Love, then, for love
of eloquence?

A fever shook my hand
that held the pen

All that – but under all
our friendship
nothing now can hide

My dear –

Enclosed: some sea pink
& a pinch of thyme

YAFFLE

The last of ebb:
Silver eeling in creeks,
Dinghies on their sides,
Cracked mudflats:

Palm, veins branching,
From which I walk.

Over deep falls,
Smelling leafmould,
Brine and dead crab,
I hear the echo
Of a laughing yaffle.

Who cares who comes
Who goes? pecker, green

Don't-give-a-damn
Woodpecker. Circling
Unseen, he laughs, drums,
Rounds all I see.

The silver between oaks
Is a ring
Gathering friends.

Deeper the echoes fathom
Sounding dugouts,
Stumps of a forest
Under peat under sea.

From woods I turn
To an estuary flooded,
Reflecting branches,
Gulls frosty against
A pale, full moon.

MONOLOGUE OF A SHELL

for David Annwn

1
Though the sea moves me
Still I wait, wait
For another to enter.

Will it follow
Aspiring snail's long crawl,
Or descend
Through polyp and medusae,
Zones of androgyne,
Down where crab protrudes its eyes,
Jellyfish pulses its bell,
Through dark, torn weed?

Or stay, where
Egg-sac and oiled, salt
Cuttle-bone lie,
Dog whelk comes with its acid,
Atoms thrive between
Irreducible grains?

Will it be
Of these kingdoms
Or another?

I wait as I must
With a patient look

2
Emptiness grows,
Sucking the residue
Of a former possessor;

Expands, draws in
Phantom sun and moon,
Shadow of earth,
Spectre of seas.

How vast
In a tiny space
The ghost of infinity.

Though I cannot bear it
Still I wait.

Without patience
I wait, mouth open
To be filled
And void my emptiness

BIRTH

I held your mother, child.
She was beyond me.

The shout forced from deep inside
Came shrill: shout
Of a body hurt and labouring
To an end: of a self lost,
Willing unwilled, giving
Delivered.
          I was not afraid
Though a storm's blue light
Flickered on steel, made the room
Tropical, dangerous.
One of the masked attendants,
I held her, beyond myself.

Hair more like seaweed on a stone
Stuck to the crown; then
A creased and slippery form
Came in a gush of blood,
More naked
Than a mussel eased from its shell,
Stranger, more ancient,
Than a creature long-drowned.

Breath came with a cry,
Earthly unearthly cry.
The knot was cut, and tied.

Outside, I watched rain drip
From railings of a balcony,
Form pools on the roof below.

Still on my wrist I feel
The reddish fluid
Where the waters breaking fell.

GULL ON A POST

Gull on a post firm
In the tideway – how I desire
The gifts of both!

Desire against the diktat
Of intellect: be single,
You who are neither.

As the useful one
That marks a channel, marks
Degrees of neap and spring;
Apt to bear jetties
Or serve as a mooring;
Common, staked with its like.

Standing ever
Still in one place,
It has a look of permanence.

Riddled with shipworm,
Bored by the gribble,
In a few years it rots.

Desire which tears at the body
Would fly unconstrained
Inland or seaward; settle
At will – but voicing
Always in her cry
Essence of wind and wave,
Bringing to city, moorish
Pool and ploughland,
Reminders of storm and sea.

Those who likened the soul
To a bird, did they ever
Catch the eye of a gull?

Driven to snatch,
Fight for slops in our wake.

Or voice a desolation
Not meant for us,
Not even desolate,
But which we christen.

Folk accustomed to sin,
Violent, significant death,
Who saw even in harbour
Signs terrible and just,
Heard in their cries
Lost souls of the drowned.

Gull stands on a post
In the tideway; I see

No resolution; only
The necessity of flight
Beyond me, firm
Standing only then.

from
ENGLISHMAN'S ROAD
1980

1 *PASSAGES*

WIND AND SHADOW

1

Day of brief rainbows
and stormy cloud.

Rain drips like dark juice
from blackberries, runs red
from hips and haws.

Where my clogged shoes
take me, wet and happy,
across the fields, under
long, skating shadows,
Hambledon darkens and gleams.

2

Ploughed fields with a scud
of white flint run high,
break at the edge.

Red fruit and yellow leaves,
beeches turning gold,
fall short.
Over the brow I can hear
continual dull thunder.

From my feet,
grass soaked dark as iron,
rounded like a planet,
the hill abruptly starts
its motionless ascent.

3

I let the wind carry me,
half asleep, like a child
who dreams of flying.

It echoes in the cave
of my head, putting out
all but a dim light.

Under my feet
which scarcely touch,
the hill flies up.

4

In the centre of the hill
I crouch.

Brilliant in shivered rays
against black cloud
a cold light falls
but does not settle.
All boundaries are open
to a race of shadows.

Against wind and shadow
the pattern holds,
ring within ring
like a banded shell.

The earth against my back
feels motionless.

In the shelter of the barrow
I rest with eyes still.

Again the rings encircle me.

IN A PLACE OF TRANSIT

1
Tongues of mud and shingle
slide away; an Esso tanker
dips towards the Gulf.

Nothing to dwell on there,
or in ground sown
with worked-out bones.

Nor can I be a channel
among the water-ways,
but must cross the new bridge
hiding the Itchen, perhaps

voicing the true relation
in a place of passage.

2
Driving out, with eyes
that never leave the road,
I feel like a slow wader,
dragging foot after lumping foot
from ooze, pulling the tide behind me.

It will cover sticks in the mud;
where I left imaginary prints
waves will spread, with a lick
of scum and a few gulls bobbing.
Now everything will be in place.

SARISBURY GREEN

Between pre-war, redbrick houses
comes a sudden break, yachts
admiring their reflections; then
the redbrick church standing
in a dark pool marked with stones.
Here are the bare bones of my people,
nor is there any thing so mean or dull
it does not bring me to the ground,
not even a strip of pavement
by a bus stop. There I enter
the body of a child, impatiently
straining against the arms
that hold him, his arms outstretched
like a swimmer's, reaching out.

2   *UNDER MYNYDD BACH, 1980*

It must be remembered that the *numina* of the hills see to the meta-
morphosis of whatever infiltrates those hills.

– David Jones

The fields are greener and the sea bluer because of the unseen
company of past generations.

– Ned Thomas, *The Welsh Extremist*

'Nor do I think, that any other nation than this of Wales, or any other
language, whatever may hereafter come to pass, shall, in the day of
severe examination before the supreme Judge, answer for this corner of
the earth.'

– Giraldus Cambrensis: the words of the old
Welshman of Pencadair to Henry II

WINTER PRELUDE

A magpie out of Brueghel
Draws his long, straight tail
Across the cold still-life;
The naked stream runs black
Below the barely parted
Overhangs of snow.
No human voice or chirrup
Where the night fall rests.

A new year, and a snowfall
Hardly marked – still
The unbelieving self is still.
I look from emptiness
Towards the covering snow.

Wales, I find below
Your silence and your sound
A silence harder than the rock
To break and deeper than the snow.

BEIDOG

Sunlight and shallow water,
rock, stones with red marks
like cuts of a rusty axe,
dark under hazel and alder,
broken white on blackened steps
and below the falls a cold pale green –
how shall I celebrate this,
    always present
under our sleep and thoughts,
where we do not see ourselves
    reflected

or know the language of memory
gathered from its fall?

Beidog running dark
   between us
and our neighbours, down
from Mynydd Bach –
this is the stream I wish to praise
   and the small mountain.

I am not of you, tongue
through whom Taliesin descends the ages
gifted with praise, who know
that praise turns dust to light.
   In my tongue,
of all arts
this is the most difficult.

SOFT DAYS AFTER SNOW

Soft days after snow,
   snowdrops
under sycamores beside the stream,
earth brown and crumbling.

Now the dark gleams softly
under catkins and water below,
alight in the February sun.
And I who desired
   eyes washed clean
as melting snow,
radiant at the point of fall,
know that every word obscures
the one I want to know.

Now soft days bear us
who take each other's hands,
and on their surface
    colder than blood
our brief appearances.

Though snowdrops follow the snow,
    and the water burns,
darkness carries them.

Our faces are taken away.

Where do you go,
    unspeakable love?

ON SAINT DAVID'S DAY

For Dewi Sant, an eye
of yellow in the daffodils,
the curlew from the sea,
the hare that lollops by a gate
    which opens wide
on far Plynlimmon,
Cader Idris
and the airy rockface
    of the northern sky.

I too would name
a tribute of these things:
cold wind,
white sun of March,
    the boundaries
whose handywork of stone
shines through the falling earth.

I turn towards the mynydd
in a film of light,
    and turning
ask of Dewi Sant
    his benediction
on these words that settle
where the uplands rise.

CURLEW

The curve of its cry –
A sculpture
Of the long beak:
A spiral carved from bone.

It is raised
    quickening
From the ground,
Is wound high, and again unwound,
    down
To the stalker nodding
In a marshy field.

It is the welling
Of a cold mineral spring,
Salt from the estuary
Dissolved, sharpening
The fresh vein bubbling on stone.

It is an echo
Repeating an echo
That calls you back.

It looses
Words from dust till the live tongue
Cry: This is mine

Not mine, this life
Welling from springs
Under ground, spiralling
Up the long flight of bone.

THE MASON'S LAW

Though the slate
where his hand slipped
could not stand
    worthy of a name,
at least it could lie
in his living room,
set in the floor.

Er Cof unfinished,
under our feet, recalls
the mason and his law:
    Honour the dead
with your craft;
waste nothing; leave
no botched memorial.

BRYNBEIDOG

For ten years the sycamores
have turned about us, the Beidog
has run with leaves, and ice and sun.
I have turned the earth, thrown up
blue chip and horseshoe; from near fields
sheep and bullocks have looked in.

We have shared weathers
with the stone house; kept its silence;
listened under winds lifting slates

for a child's cry; all we have
the given space has shaped, pointing
our lights seen far off
as a spark among scattered sparks.
    The mountain above
has been rock to my drifting mind.

Where all is familiar, around us
the country with its language
gives all things other names;
there is darkness on bright days
and on the stillest a wind
that will not let us settle,
but blows the dust from loved
things not possessed or known.

WIND BLEW ONCE

Wind blew once till it seemed
the earth would be skinned from the fields,
the hard roots bared.
    Then it was again
a quiet October,
red berries on grey rock
and blue sky, with a buzzard crying.

I scythed half-moons in long grass,
with nettle-burn stinging my arms,
bringing the blood's rhythm back.
    At night
in our room we lay in an angle
between two streams,
with sounds of water meeting,
    and by day

118

the roads ran farther,
joined and formed a pattern
at the edge of vast, cloudy hills.

   The house was small
against the mountain; from above,
a stone on a steep broad step
of falling fields; but around us
the walls formed a deep channel,
with marks of other lives, holding
its way from worked moorland
to this Autumn with an open sky.

COMMON LAND ABOVE TREFENTER

This is no haunt
For the painter of prospects.

Sheep will not bleat a complaint
Or the barn owl hoot derision,
Where poverty abounded
Providing shelter.

On bared common, where
Nocturnal migrants homed,
There is room for the kite
Cleaned out of cities, none
For the import of terror,

For alien shadow
In common daylight,
Or fashion
Of nightmare or grandeur:

Thin cawl
On the valley's bread line
Is not its provider, nor
Dwellings built in a night,
Fields wide as an axe throw
From the door, patterning
Moorland with stony patches.

Only the bare history
Under foot – holdings

Untenable, falling back
Into quarries; last post
Of hedge-bank craftsmen,
With breast plough and mattock,
On the road to the coalface.

HILL COUNTRY RHYTHMS
for Robert Wells

Sometimes I glimpse a rhythm
I am not part of, and those who are
could never see.
   The hawk I disturb
at his kill, leaving bodiless,
bloody wings spread, curves
away and with a sharp turn
follows the fence; and the fence
lining a rounded bank flies
smoothly downhill, then rises
to wind-bowed trees whose shape
the clouds take on, and the ridge
running under them, where
the sky bears round in a curve.
On the mountainside stands
a square white farm, its roof

a cutting edge, but it too
moves with shadow and cloud.
  I glimpse this
with the hawk in view, lose it
to fenceposts and trees holding
a still day down, and wings
dismembered at my feet, while
down the road comes a neighbour
singing loudly, with his herd
big-uddered, slowly swaying.

AS A THOUSAND YEARS

Not a soul, only
a stubble field, bales
like megaliths; a flight
of trees over the Beidog,
and behind, darker green,
at the back of the sky,
the ridge damming
the sun; then,
  for a breath,
there was no sign of us.
Not a soul, only
light flooding this field,
bright as a marigold.

IN A WELSH PRIMARY SCHOOL
for Mari Llwyd

Around me, elements
of this place form a world,
with dragons, flowers,
flying houses on the walls;
shepherds with real crooks

and kings with tinsel crowns.
Here I also come to learn,
and know the same care
Gwion knows, Aled, Ifor
and the rest; and glimpse
through mist between
two languages,
the kindest things of Wales.

Mari, though I stand outside,
may I be numbered still
with all who give you praise.

A NEIGHBOUR

I remembered his laugh – once
he almost fell from a chair;
also with one hammerblow
he drove a fencepost in.
Some weeks I saw only him,
with his dogs and stick, old coat
and greasy cap, walking
from the mountain to his fields;
and we talked – we said aye
to everything, with a language
between us, and rare china
civility, out in wind, rain or sun.
He was first to welcome us,
standing in the door saying aye, aye . . .

I would have seen him then,
strangely white, thinning the hedge
with a hook, his old coat hung on a branch;
but instead a flock of starlings
turned me aside – a swirl

of black flecks over the valley.
Then, seeing the graveyard,
I did not look again
at the hedge, with white, jagged ends.

SHEPHERD

Others have died or left;
he has grown louder, bigger,
filling the fields which he keeps
with an old skill.

I picture him through glass,
framed in the window,
against the mountain:

tall, strongly made,
ruddy from wind and sun,
a man who strides, sings,
waves a stick, then shouts
at his dogs with a voice
they will hear in the village.

And he turns, walks
through the frame, as he has
since he came as a boy
and stood with his father
saying aye, aye . . .

PWYLL THE OLD GOD

'I would be glad to see a wonder,' said Pwyll
'I will go and sit on the hill.'

The Mabinogion

Pwyll the old god
may look through you,
when you look through eyes
of spiderwebs, through
tiny rainbows brilliant
as bluebottle shards, and see,
in a dance of gold flecks,
the mountain hang by a strand.

This may be his emblem:
a ram's skull with a thread
of silk between its horns,
but certainly you see
the everyday, the wonder:

Old windblown light
fresh as this morning;
rooks with black breasts
and silver backs; clear-cut
shadows brightening fields,
and over the ridge the sun,
curve of a dark body
in blinding white; everywhere
fragments of web shining,
that look like ends.

EMILY

The season is late; our long shadow
with two clothes peg heads notched
one above the other lies flat across the field;
and from above me, breaking
the quiet of sleepy baas and caws,
an excited voice exclaims
at a sudden vision:
    a yellow digger

uprooting bushes, changing the stream's
meanders to a straighter course.

Now our single track divides,
a dark fork in dew-grey grass,
and a small girl in a red frock,
sun yellowing her fair hair, runs
away from me with a bunch
of corn marigolds, campion,
harebells and a magpie feather
crushed in her fist.

Away she runs through a drift
of thistledown, seeds
stuck to her bare wet legs;
runs away laughing, shouting
for me to catch her –
but I know now that I never will;
      never, my darling;
but run with care, run lightly
with the light about you,
run to the gate through moist soft grass,
webs and bright blades all about you,
      hint of a rainbow
in the silver shower at your heels.

LINES TO A BROTHER
to Tony Hooker

Waking early today,
I think of you preparing
for work, driving through
a quiet Oxfordshire dawn.

You will join
sawn timbers, intimate
as their owners will never be
with roof-tree and joist,
while I lie awake, watching
light form the bulk of Mynydd Bach.

I see your hands,
steadied by the recreation
of labour, and again
the morning air tastes thin;
once more I turn
to images of the skilled life
we have drawn from and shared,
in whose absence
my words offer no habitation.

BEHIND THE LIGHTS

Last night, I looked from the Island.
Then I was again
behind the lights, living there
blindly, where the mainland
long shore shone, with breaks
at Forest and river mouths,
a ghostly smoke round chimneys;
till suddenly, a green light
on black water cut across my view.

Tonight, I return
to another darkness, the house
strangely cold; behind me
the long road back to Wales.
It will be dark in an hour
but now the sun setting
picks out a fox in the field

above the house, cutting across my view.
There he goes gingerly,
a lordly fox, golden red.
  Tired, I see
a green light on black water.
  Better to follow the fox,
from sunlight into shadow,
on his cold way home.

PRAYER IN JANUARY

Now when the old New Year
Starts red with sun on snow,
Must resolution splinter
Like a frosted bough?
The stars of ancient January
Hurt the eyes; by day, like stars,
Snow crystals make them ache.
But Yahweh's eyes burn clear
As drops that fall from alders
By the mountain stream.
They are not stars or melting snow
But outstare every star
And every thing most star-like
In this old, cold, flaming universe.

Soft heart, small, bitter pool
Beneath your darkening hemisphere
Of ice, hidden eyes blaze
Where you hide. Regard
Their hard regard, that weighs
The worth of all you guard
At not a fraction of its price.
Let love outlast such love
As self, too tender of itself,
Has dreamed regardless of a sight

More pitiless, more pitiful than you.
Then be unselved, or drying
When the eyes burn through
Die dreamless into hard-ribbed clay.

SYCAMORE BUDS

Then speak, not
from the shell of self,
its beaten walls, but
as these pointed buds
with tight, green scales
the winter could not loose
and waste the rising force
erecting spikes, that
lengthen, curving
into soft, closed beaks
that open on their tongues
and now unfold small hands:
wrinkled, blood-red leaves,
fresh and glistening
damp – shapes of the force
they are, containing them.

DRAGONS IN THE SNOW

Thaw to the hedgerows
left white crosses on the hill;
    the first thrush sang.

Now a buzzard cries, confirming
    silence under all.

The few bare trees are darker
for the fall that covers
    boundaries,
and in their place reveals
contrasting absolutes.

We are so small,
the boy and I, between
the snowclouds and the snow.

He starts from here,
who talks of dragons
as we walk, the first today
to leave a human sign
beside the marks of sheep and crow.

He warms me
with confiding hand
and fiery talk,
    who also start
upon the ground
of choice, the silence
answering the choice;
happy to be small, and walk,
and hear of dragons in the snow.

LEAVING

Against the wall
a boy's bike leans
waiting for its rider.

I look from the stream
through a sycamore –
breakfast things on the table
wait in place;

vapour trails shine
like ruts in the sky
on airways far to the south.

Sun on the ridge.
The house filled with light.

For the first time
it is hollow, echoing,
the living room
cavernous.

As I walk away
the Beidog winds, gleaming –
joining field to field.

I climb and the sea rises,
silver, a planet's rim;
peak climbs on peak,
blue and far,

the house settles –
smaller, deeper, in place.

Do we simply
pack ourselves away?
The hearth's a black hole
where you knelt.

After days of storm,
fallen slates, fields
grey with exhaustion,
buzzards come, and a kite
picking red slivers,

a ewe shelters lambs
at the lattice of a thorn.

Floors skinned,
picture shapes on walls,
in each doorway
a shock of cold.

Under hills clouded,
bent backed,
I crumble black earth
through fingers
caked with earth:

ground worked
over and over, where
we too grow round
with windbreak sycamores.

Just now
I put out my hand
for a table, which this morning
I broke up and burnt

and nearly fell,
nearly leant on its rim.

Midsummer silence falls,
the dry lanes smell
of dog roses and dust.

Foxgloves snake from hedgerows,
a buzzard circles mewing
round and round.

I lie down,
dash the stream in my face,
look up at the slate roof
tilted against the ridge.

Bare, flesh coloured boards.
Briefly
in childless quiet
the house waits

from ENGLISHMAN'S ROAD
for Peter Lord

Take a long view from Mynydd Bach: let your eye rise and fall with ridges that stone walls or bent thorns follow – green dragon backs, crested like petrified breakers; yet also the walls are always climbing or in flight.

This is a country of vast spaces: it rolls with hidden hollows to the mountains of the north, against the sweep of sea –

> preternatural grey,
> the mountains of Llŷn
> a chain of islands
> or blue as spirit flame,
> or a lunula of beaten gold.

Here the buzzard with broad wings spread draws a widening circle, ringing an intricate pattern of commons and enclosures, whitewashed farms and red-roofed barns.

At night an irregular pattern of lights reflects the stars.

Here the western light is always changing, too quick for the eye though it notes

> grey mystery
> of April, haunted
> by the curlew's salty cry,
> or August
> floating the hills,

or Winter
with a hard whiteness
hammering the ground.

And what the light changes is only a face – face of a work vaster and
more laboured than the pyramids; but continuing. For this is settled
country, its pattern absorbent, deeply ingrained, but unfinished; without
the finality of a coiled fossil, though it too is a life wrought in rock. And
here these English words play on a surface through which they cannot
shine, to illumine its heart; they can possess the essence of this place no
more than the narrow road under the Welsh mountain can translate its
name.

Lon Sais it is called,
not Englishman's Road.

['Englishman's Road' was a poem for radio]

from
MASTER OF THE LEAPING FIGURES
1987

MASTER OF THE LEAPING FIGURES

Under his hand the great book
glows with lapis lazuli, red,
gold, and in the smoke
of fire-balls falling on the city.

Outside, the torturer's art:
figures hung up by the thumbs,
jerking on a blackened ground.
Devils fill the castles, and the people
reel in a divided land, fleeing
from the horsemen; peasants
are forced from the fields
to drag carts loaded with stone,
and the crops rot.
Men say openly that Christ
and His saints sleep.

Under his hand, they do not sleep.
Here he is master,
illuminating the Word in a little letter,
painting in a tiny space
the beginning and the end.

Lines cut deep in time
meet in his hand: from Rome,
Byzantium, Ireland
and the Viking north;
from tracks hacked through woodland
and seaways marked by wrecks;
from monks of the Saxon minster,
a ruin outside the workshop.

It is not love of violence
that leaps in the figures,
but violent love:
David gripping the lion's jaw;
Moses clubbing the Egyptian,
as a Saxon remembering his home
might dream of smashing the skull
of his conqueror;
Christ thrusting the devil into Hell.

All flame against the dark,
like the prophet who is one
fire with the horses of fire,
blazing against the blue
of a midsummer night-sky
with a rim of gold;
a man barely contained
by the frame holding him
who leaps in flesh of flame
in a world on fire, burning
in the mantle that he passes on.

from A WINCHESTER MOSAIC

The great Ethelwold
ordered a certain monk
to write the present book.
He commanded also to be made
many frames well adorned
and filled with curious figures
decorated with gold.

Let all who look upon this book
pray always
that I may abide in heaven.
Godeman, the scribe,
earnestly asks this.

Looking up in Nuns Road
I am startled to see

the head of a young man
framed at an upper window
in lamp light, studying,

and in him, in his
intentness, other
figures – scribes, and one
I have long dreamed of,
listening, seeing
with the eyes of the place.

I stand for a moment
watching him,
in a stillness
of dusk-red brick,
the houses statuesque.

At the top of the road,
high in a tree over the stream,
a thrush is singing.

★

Delight wakes in the day
with the daisies, the day's eyes
lifted after frost.

A sycamore, bark flaking
in scales of mossy green and grey,
bares an orange skin.
A fork stuck in a dunghill
wears an old blue bucket
like a hat.

Already the sun is everywhere,
brightest where caught
and broken in a mallard's wake.

The trees of the park
are naked dancers –
not a tremor, only the poise
before the first, slow movement.

★

Twice today it has happened –
cherry blossom scattering
pink and white on the breeze:
walking by the cathedral walls
I have passed a woman,
and entered a cloud of perfume
so strong, so sweet
I almost fell
against the odourless cold stone.

★

In clumps of celandines
sharp petals strain wide
to hold and consume the sun.

Beaked horse-chestnut buds
stretch out, sticky
from reddish brown sheaths.

I notice in faces of passers-by
the life in each, held back
or partially risen; in men

a flushed sensuality.
I cultivate observation,
shameless with strange women.

*

A smell of cut grass and growing nettles.
Ducklings, hatched a week ago
that boldly range the bourne.

Among lime trees, the pale yellow
of a solitary street lamp left on,
dying in the light of leaves.

An old lady dressed in brown
who showers bread to a circle
of ducks pressed against her feet

and draws me in with her
'Aren't they nice?' as she turns
a delighted, open face.

*

Old stories
repeat themselves –

the 'oldest resident'
cradled in chalk
at a motorway interchange;
or a man unearths
Roman coins in the cellar
of his Victorian house,
and in his garden
a stone-carved, Saxon head –

Every day
something new.

★

Too late repeats
the train in the
cutting too
late twitter
small, green birds
on branches
budding over
carriage roofs
too late.

★

We ripped down
the hands of strangers,
we scraped pain into the walls.

Gradually the house appeared:

bare boards,
patched and flaking plaster –
broken timber and a small, dusty frog.

For days I scraped mindlessly
till my head ached,
refusing to see
what must fill the space.

★

An old man passes slowly.
He is bent over, pushing
an old woman in a wheelchair.

Effort strains his face
but they are talking together
quietly, easily.

★

There is no more bitter taste:

I have seen a devil pictured
in a man's mouth,
the same mouth
that was moist with love.

★

Wind moulds the cloud
into great bowls,
which slowly lose shape,
curling and flaking.

Below, a curve
of the land, a line
clear as a pencil stroke
except for a clump of trees
on a downland ridge
far across the city –
a small dark clump, and two
minute dark figures
walking together along the line.

★

Red brick glows
through the lime trees'
light, cool leaves.
My children run with the dog
chasing swallows.

Dog bark, shout,
echoing strokes
of cathedral bell.

143

I too once lived here
I shall say.

★

In this scene
all things are one
in a fiery light,
between yellow stormcloud
and a cornfield's darkening gold.

Steam with the curl of stooks,
the mass of cloudy leaves,
rises from a train
hidden deep in the cutting.

Chimneys and flint gables
stand out in a corner –
where this morning, from flats
obscuring the harvesters' view,
demolition notices could be seen,
and workmen lighting fires in
                              the garden.

★

The sightseer comes suddenly
on a mirror facing the roof,
looks down, and staggers.
The floor has opened,
he reels at a cliff edge.

Slowly the depths settle,
forming a strange world:

Roof bosses,
like rock pool anemones,
far down on the stone bed;
choir stall stalactites;

144

a cross hanging
upsidedown, drowned
in a meer of light –

which becomes the well
of a great, stone-ribbed ship;
which he has passed through
on his pilgrimage,
and not sighted; in which
he will not voyage.

★

Tall pillars sway. Sunlight lies yellow on worn steps.

A boy's well-bred voice flutes: 'And the light shineth in
darkness'.
A master's voice responds: 'Not intense enough; more
enthusiasm'.

The stillness is a held tension of violent cross-currents,
race against race.

Centuries in this place have put on the armour of stone:
painted giant bishops; cadavers; a crusader with the face
of a battered pugilist; aldermen and riflemen. Sir Redvers
Buller sounds a poetry of empire in bronze: Ashanti,
Red River, China . . .

It is he who has made us and not we ourselves.

Names and dates in stone: Adrian Battin 1608 W Hinton 1787
Charlie Lightfoot ER 1582 Vicky Milly Walter. In every corner, on
almost every flagstone, a sign of life. Then the tomb closes, is a history, a
style.

John Keats loiters in the aisle reading a love letter.

★

They came with blood and light
in their eyes, where
'The Powers that be
are ordained of God'.

They broke in the doors.
They entered with drums beating;
behind the troopers
horsemen rode up the aisles.

They hacked at statues.
They smashed the altar
and gashed the Virgin.
They threw down chests,

jumbling bones of bishops
with bones of Saxon kings.
Skulls grinned at them,
level with their feet.

They saw the joke, and took
thigh bones and flung them
against the west window,
shattering the Resurrection.

The blast that scattered
harlot amethyst and rose
let in pure light, and air
their souls could breathe.

★

Shall these bones live?

Shall the living
who die to each other?

★

Jerome, restorer
of broken images,
paints the choir stalls.

Outside
the world shrinks from highways
and pestilent streets
to the household doors.

A neighbour carrying
comfort to neighbours
may strike them down.

Twilight lays a gold rod
on Jerome's handiwork,
which he leaves,

and goes home, and gathers
his wife and children together
in the inner room.

★

A flower
on Pompeian red
which someone looked at
waking or making love.

A dolphin
out of its element.

Bones and teeth
of labourers
telling their diseases.

A mummified heart.

The 'Castle'
seeming to float

on surface over surface,
in a November dusk
of dim violet and faded rose –

behind a wall
of lit windows, clerks
administering to us,
filing case-histories.

★

He records facts:

Born in 1899, in Upper Brook Street.
Sailor in the Princess Royal
at the Battle of Jutland.
Cook on the Mauritania.
Window cleaner.

He remembers, when
he and his wife moved in,
cattle were driven to market
up North Walls – now
a defile for through traffic.

He saw an escaped bull
stuck fast in a doorway,
trapping a man behind a table.
'What a mess, there was blood everywhere.'

He recalls the kindness
of an undertaker,
who would visit the dying
with a jug of soup.
'Good for business you see.'

When Upper Brook Street
had a brook, he fell in,

and ruined his only suit,
and missed his brother's wedding.

Since his wife died
he has lived alone
in the same house, in a row
due for demolition.
'There's still love in my life.'

★

Some days I sense
a whole design even
in the meanest shard,
and in dust
a great company
at the edge of sight.

Then at night I stand
at a curtainless window,
with only my face beside
the skeletal moon
of a paper lightshade
hanging in the dark.

★

I make this memorial

for Lucretianus,
who dedicated an altar
of blue sandstone
to the Italian, German,
Gallic and British Mothers;

and for Athelwine,
who founded St Peter
in the Flesh Shambles
in memory of his parents.

Though their works are numbered
among broken things,
time does not waste a gift
that opens the heart.

★

I LOVE JENNY EASTWOOD
someone has chalked
on the church path.

The letters in stone
nearby have weathered
a hundred and fifty years:

IN MEMORY OF
JANE WIFE OF
JOHN SWITZER

Their stones lean together
against the churchyard fence.
She was sixteen when she died.

The message is plain,
and perhaps untrue.
I know nothing
of love's time –

but it is not
the duration of stone
or a shower of rain.

May Jenny love you too,
whoever you are.

★

My mind has slowed
to the rhythm of the words.

150

There is now no more
to be thought or said.

They came as a gift
in the empty house,
unwired, half-decorated,
where I knelt in the light
of a gas fire breathing
dust from the carpet,
wiping dust from the dial
to see the number to ring:

the only strength is love.

★

A vague pale yellow full moon
shows through a grey sky.
As I walk, it snows, at first
a few small flakes, like ash
from a distant bonfire.
Then a steady windless fall.
It is a dream in which I see
the scholar's lamp shining
by his empty chair.
I could walk on in this for ever.

I SAW THE WALLS OF AVEBURY

Raised sarsens shaped
like giant hand-axe or torso,
carved flanks of a curving earth,
compelled the feet in a dance,
embraced village and cranesbill;
sheep rubbed against the stones
and a church stood among them,
on its wall a hand-carved Christ.

He was no victor in the ring
with fire and sledgehammer,
but a lover raising
his fallen bride; a dark wind
blasting in the circle
flowed through his hands.
Then I saw on the skyline ridge
fragments of an outer wall. Far round
domed beech crowns turned, and white
ancestral fields of Wiltshire
streamed and eddied with a sky
whose reach was fathomless.
But the voice of an impotent love
rasped in my heart – What use
this dance in a ring with the dead?
I saw the walls of Toxteth
and Brixton – desecrated
smashed brickwork – and the walls
we crack against, manufactured
in the brain, constructed through speech,
dividing us cell from cell –
brothers only in a common death.

IN MEMORY OF DR CHARLES HOPE GILL

Who now will touch these men
and make them whole?
No one will say of this man, 'father'
or of the other, '*his* father'.

He has left them speechless,
alone in the frame.
They are specimens in the cage of history.
His death makes them a death's head.

★

152

You are not with your fathers yet,
though today I uncover parts of you:

> schoolboy in tasselled cap,
> officer in regimental buttons,
> doctor with instruments,
> birdwatcher, sailor, photographer.

★

I have come here to continue
a conversation about death

but death has ended it.
'I shall not know when I die,' you said.

And after?
Here is the point we never got beyond.

I have come here again today,
and wait, half expecting a reply.

★

This is his chair.
I feel it holds him still, and print
his shape on air. Briefly
it might – if any image
in my mind were him at all.

Dead, he is only a picture
of shrunken clay: a moment
in a dream, that sees
the coffin launched towards the fire.

★

Everything that remains
is not you. In this room
close with your dying,

the well worn and the long known
fall apart. You are whole
in no place, broken in our minds.

No word of mine
will hold you back. Let me
rather let you go, free
from our fearful and dying bodies,
sailing out from the hard
to your hide on a shingle island
and the terns you catch always in flight.

ON A CHILD'S PAINTING

1
We three play in our garden.

I am reddest red
and the yellow sun's no bigger, no brighter.
Nor are we smaller or bigger than the tree
which has landed at my feet:
        a green anchor.

I stand looking up with my red eye.
We three are the world:
        the tree

                the sun

                        and me.

2
Each spider moves enclosed
at the centre of its circle.
The water spins with wheels and shadows
and at the bottom
the sky lies white among branches.

A carving on slate could not be more distinct.
Sunlight through trees
quivers, and its beams on the river bed
bend, and are gold.

But you, small and naked, come
smashing the image to glassy splinters,
with a green leaf stuck to your heel.

FOR JOHN RILEY

Consider also a channel:

image open to the end
leaving no sadness

of mud closed in
and maze of creeks, but

a wind freshening
through banks clear cut

to a river mouth, open
where light streams in

from ITCHEN WATER
for David Sherlock
and Winchester School of Art

When I stand dully
slopping at the dam
of self and the river
dashes it away,
may I give back

of all the river gives
one ripple or one wave,
one chalk-grey grain,
or in a word alive
with light, one drop
in which its nature shines.

ABOVE THE ITCHEN VALLEY

Here we either fly,
sweeping over down after down
and with the domed clouds,
or are rooted to the earth
at our feet, turning over
a mountainous flint,
sliding from a fold
of its chalkface
to the great downs
of an August sky,
a smudge of blue smoke –
Southampton, and the sea.

Here are ragwort so hot
it hurts to look at them.
There a skyline of bales
like Avebury sarsens;
the half-burnt beech clump
of Cheesefoot Head.
With sweat in my eyes
I see all gone.
Then rest amazed on an oak
rising from crackling wheat,
its shadow crown
an island in the blaze.

AT THE SOURCE
for Norman Ackroyd

1 The Source

A small pool in undergrowth,
too hidden to mirror the sky,
in which we alone may see
liners plunge in the ocean,
villages and cities
growing on the banks,
or even the small stream
several fields away, gathering
for the course through a history
it does not witness,
though to us standing beside it
nothing seems more like an eye
that sees everything to come.

2 Cheriton Long Barrow

A long low hill in a hill field,
a curve within a curve,
white of ploughed chalk
on pale arable: epitome
of winter's purity and grace,
of lines like the skeleton's
long since at one with its bed,
and with nothing opposing it
but the first violet
barely visible in the open hedge.

3 Civil War Battlefield

Over the hill the land opens
deceptively and a mound
covers Hopton's raw men
and Waller's troopers.

The few hedgerow oaks
are motionless, as the storm
of another season builds
slowly in their trunks.
Flints picked from the fields
look like corpses flung in a heap.
There is no sound but rooks
returning to their rookery
on the battleground,
ewes, and lambs born today
that totter all bloody
to drink their mothers' milk.

GANDER DOWN

The ploughed chalk sweeping
and shelving is a shore
from which the tide has just gone out.

Fine, black blades
of trees stand against depths
which the sun fills,
white and cold.

A big hare sits with ears up
on the rim of the world.

Larks rise singing from the ocean bed.

TICHBORNE

*to Chidiock Tichborne (1558–86), executed
for his part in the Babington Plot*

There is no place deeper in earth –
where the young quick river grows

and cressy streams feed it
on beds of purest chalk stones;
and the rhythms of settlement
remember a life before his,
from Vernal Farm through meadow,
copse and ploughland, and St Andrews
standing against curve and swell,
where Catholic and Protestant
share a roof, and members
of his family who succeeded him
figure in stone.
His place is not with those
who gained the world.
Nor can there be an elegy
for one who wrote his own:
the perfect balance
of a man who would soon be
'bowelled alive and seeing'.
About to die, his claim
was a faithful occupation
older than the Normans;
a long life before him here,
which he planted again
on the scaffold, in Tichborne earth.

AT OVINGTON
for Lee Grandjean, sculptor

You would make a form
that contains, which your hand moulds
as we talk, creating a body
between us, in the air. Below
the broad full river glides
hypnotically, silver,
green and dark. Here wind
meets light and water,

and the current at each instant
finds its bed, erupting
over shoals of weed, sliding
through a lucid gravel run,
continually making
and unmaking lines,
as in my mind I catch
and loose its images,
and about our heads
swifts hawking for mayfly
unerringly, explosively, glide.
I would let all go again,
saying – it is perfect without us,
but we meet here, we share
words and your hand shaping
the flow, the brute
and graceful wings.
And our feet beat solidly on the bridge.

AVINGTON: THE AVENUE AT DAWN

A leaf sways gently on a web.
Herons reveal the hidden river
slowly where they fly.
Mist creeps over the barley.
Time to get up, stiffbacked
from our damp sleeping bags,
where we have trespassed.
Time for the avenue to show
where we are, on a carriage drive
of nettles and grass,
that leads back through memories
of landscaped order: wheels
brushing the trimmed foliage
and the master at the centre

of his park, where the limes
near death are wild giants
now; and abruptly ends
at a gateway crumbling
in undergrowth. Across the lane
a new entrance, young limes
sweeping to the big house.
Here a lonely grey horse
careers across a field,
and quivering in front of us,
stares at the strangers.

SPRING MOVEMENTS

1 May Morning

Misty leafy morning, green and grey,
with a blackbird on a white branch –
as if the image were all
and I their composer.
His call corrects me,
his whimpering notes, repeated,
a message perhaps to fledglings:
Take care Take care Take care
But to me now the sound of fulness.

Cherry blossom in the first spring
returned to Hiroshima.
Here it is on the air and on the ground
and still the branches are pink and white.
All is effortless power,
a giant chestnut lifts a mass of candles.
The eyes of the dead were everywhere

Children cross a bridge above me,
their silhouettes skip and dance,
flat and dark against the light.
From here they might belong to any time,
generation tumbling on the heels of generation

But I am too far away to see,
when I come near they are too real
beginning this misty leafy morning

2 Nuns Walk

New morning. Shadows of June grass
curve and sway on a tarmac path.
They are blown the way of the bourne,
that runs to dark under a chestnut.
Moorhens, neat and bright,
with chicks dizzy from the egg, circle.
What else? Habit like shadow
sweeping a path it does not touch?
With eyes closed I can imagine
anything, but think – Each
is locked in his life and death.

Mother of God. My Lord. Nothing,
nothing is here, only water,
waterbirds, windblown grass.
Easily I could raise a ghost,
in robe of dusty light, walking
from a book. I know inside me
a snivelling child.

They do not walk, but walked once,
and have gone, as each must go
leaving another day, others
twisting their bead of self,
calling on kindness to bear them.

Only, perhaps,
one turned from himself
might sense another, prayer
running into prayer,
and walk alone, sharing the day.

WINTER MOVEMENTS

1 St Swithun's Bridge

I recall
at Swithun's bridge
his humble miracle –
smashed eggs made whole
for an old woman. Where
the Itchen surges from Water Lane
through City Mill and races
by the medieval wall,

his faith was like a great mill wheel –
made for use in the power
of love; like the ducks
that are everyday, and use
the current at their will.

Now only the same new river
moves, fullbodied, swift and pure.
All other things are still.
Gardens of snow,
almost immaculate.
Ivy with fruit of ice.
Alders wasting their seed.

2 The Weirs: In Snow

The shadowed river dark as flint
breaks out, racing in the sun –

The gravity of time
in this stone mortuary
is now perhaps
    a blinding wave
    a crystal dance
    an atom of the cold pure air.

Now over Wolvesey's battlements
the Cathedral tower is a ghost.
Meadows and College fields
are one white lawn
under St Catherine's Hill.

Snow puffs from a yew where a bird
lands dying for warmth.

Now time in this place turned to stone
is light perhaps

and death a living word.

ATLANTIC SPRING

Spring touches the river softly
with thistledown, willow flowers,
gauzy insects – tiny propellers
that will not be airborne again.

But the boys break it. For them
it is a game, a wild game,
as they leap whooping into tyres
or paddle stealthily from the bank
that is England
to the island in midstream.
They will panic the ducks
on South Georgia,
churn the chalk stream muddy grey.
Every splash is fifty men dead.

When the warm wind gusts
a snowstorm of blossom
whites out cricketers in the park.
And now, watchers and players,
all might be figures
in an Edwardian paperweight –
the preserved
of a cathedral city
whose round hills under the dome
of sky keep us from time.
A dream that follows the river
to the coast, whose very air
is silt, where
the stone axe lies with the spitfire.

Suddenly nostalgia possesses its desire:
troopships depart from playgrounds,
destroyers from scrapyards;
we are fearless, intrepid, invincible.
In the silence after hooters,
the voice of Vera Lynn.

Families hoarse and red-eyed
at dockhead hold closer,
each round an absent man.

I too walk in a dream,
watching white petals drown,
and see again the desolate,
embattled zones of childhood:
Fareham, Gosport, Pompey,
estates where there is hardly a man
and the women wait.
As in Argentina they wait,
over the winter sea that must,
before summer, bereave them, or numb them,
and freeze us harder in our glassy sphere.

THE DIVER

*to William Walker, whose work on the foundations of Winchester
Cathedral from 1906 to 1911 saved the building*

1

This was a great cross, shaken,
an ancient decaying tree.
A foundering ship, breaking her back,
Titanic of the watermeadows –
except for him.

He descended each day
to the pitch of death.
Enshrined stillness, turbulence of prayer,
rested on him.

In darkness, with dockyard skill,
he made the foundations sound.

And rose through the graveyard each evening.

2

He rises here still.

He is The Diver:
fish bowl and goggle eyes.
More weird, friendlier, than a mason's monster.
Ropes and pre-war innocence
hang about him.
His globe swims through chaos.
He walks alive among the dead.

He stands here too,
with builders whose face he saved:
a workman offering his hands.

A CHILD ON ST CATHERINE'S HILL

Lightly she scoops up
the city in her arms.
Even the winter sky
shares her mood, as it cracks,
scatters silver
over watermeadows,
strikes gold
from the Hampshire hog
of the Castle weathervane.
She sweeps in
footballers running rings
on green squares; racing
boats crawling on the canal;
the Cathedral
at the centre, like a model
centuries of builders
will perfect; all things
that daily enclose us
between the flint
and the red brick walls.
She can reach the downs
far round, the coast, the blue
gasometers of Northam,
and hug it all for a moment,
and lightly let it go.

ST CROSS
for Jeffrey Wainwright

1
Over the footworn step,
between old walls
that have soaked in
river-damp, in
the twilight nave,

there is something
that is not ourselves.

Something to grasp
if we could name it;
like the tile
with its legend:
                    Have mynde

2
The damp, still dusk
of December breaks,

and light sweeps the aisle
slowly, bringing back
grey sky, grey stone:

                    St Cross
signing the valley
with a man's power
and his penitence,
mindful of
Henry of Winchester,
soldier-bishop,
turning from the world.

3
The light as it passes
reveals an old woman
kneeling at altar rails
of a side chapel.

No ghost, but one
completely given;
as if the body of stone
had formed round her,
and she would be here
after it has gone.

ITCHEN NAVIGATION

What I love is the fact of it.

A channel kept open, shipping
stone for the cathedral;
blue Cornish slates;
coal from Woodmill
to Blackbridge wharf.

A channel used, disused,
restored, until the last barge
passed under the railway bridge,
now abandoned, framing
water that is going nowhere,
but silts, with passages
the colour of stonedust
and boys rowing, a surface
silver and boiling
where blades dip and turn.

It is the stillness
afterwards, grey water
settling back to the shape
of slow working journeys
during a thousand years.

WOODMILL

1
Held back, the quick chalk stream
is almost killed. Black-green,
with a gleam of dull silver,
the water reflects a tangle of branches
and ivied trunks; a doll's pram
and skeletal wheels are drowned

at the edge. Farther back,
a greasy film smooths out
eddies and ripples, and the surface
whitens, like an eye going blind.

2
Below the mill, the tide at once
greens the walls and every thing
it reaches; bladder-wrack
floating under water touches
the surface with brown fingers.
There are boats at garden ends,
a solitary shipwright's oak
among poplars and hawthorns
on the riverside walk. Roofs
of the town rise above the river
in sharp, red waves, and the water
runs with gulls on its back,
and a smell of salt and mud.

CROSSING THE NEW BRIDGE

As we crossed the new bridge
you looked through it,
through the view of ships
and oil tanks, and saw
a gravel track, the floating-bridge,
your father with a pony and trap
on the shore. And you said,
'he wouldn't know the place
if he could come back now'.

Later, on the shore, you spoke
of him and of your mother,
of being young and in love
and feeling you could walk

on moonlight on the water,
with a man who died long ago;
you spoke, too, of friends
long-dead, and of your brother,
the uncle I never knew.

You looked through near things,
but not into distance.
The man with the trap, the children,
all the people with you,
were real as the shingle and the sun,
and for me the shore
was firm again as it was
at first, when you said,
'they're part of us, we're part of them'.

INSCRIPTION FOR THE POETRY OF HORSES
for my mother

I give this
in memory of the shires
of your childhood,
who were ploughed down
in the mud of the Somme,
and left their invisible bulk
heavy in the half-light
of a Hampshire stable
and their brass medals
to furnish saloons
at The Waggon and The Ploughman.

I give this for those
who left you the echo
of hoof-falls, memories
of a playground in their shadow,
of earth that has their shape:

movers of earth,
earth-bearers, slow sure
teachers of patience,
gentleness and strength –
foundations
of your father's house.

CLAUSENTUM

I have walked
from purist's dryfly stream
to ramshackle tidal reach,
used and reused
in commerce with the sea,
and at last, secretive
at the heart of the city,
the Roman port.

    Clausentum:
    the long-imagined
    where I come now
    for the first time.

And find a grassy hard,
two girls sunbathing,
a boy riding his bike;
and blue water, homely
with houseboats,
a popular tune drifting
from the other shore.

    Clausentum:
    like the feel
    of shingle; like
    the first word.

And I am glad
there is no sign of Rome;
nothing to disturb
the legionary still
intact in my mind.
No matter if he did not lie
whole and fully armed
in Northam mud.

WESTON SHORE

Cranes in a misty light
lean delicately,
towering over dockhead.
Abbey ruins and oil tanks
look soft and vague.

There are nautical ropes
hanging from live branches,
and a white trunk,
bark skinned off, its hollow
a nest of dead-white stones.

★

We hold first things
in our hands, or touch them:
cockle shells, ship's timber,
bladder-wrack, stones.

These are gifts I give my children,
and receive from them –
except the shepherd's crown
we do not find.

★

The channel magnifies
engine noises – hydrofoil,
ferry, small gunboat.
All insist on this surface,
now, today's business.
But under the tideway
other waters are running.
There the first sailor puts out;
deeper still the first land.

★

The tide at last goes out
suddenly from the shingle,
exposing pipelines, rows of posts,
a stretch of pebbles and mud.
We are smaller now,
and the bait-diggers venturing out
are tiny, almost lost
like pea-sized crabs at our feet,
against the estuary and farther shore.

★

I do not want to say *back,*
I want to tread the word
into the stones.

I want it to be the stones
and my footfall,
where they join.

Oystercatchers picking at
the tideline, the gulls
that miss no scrap,
have no more right than mine.

NETLEY: ON THE SITE OF THE ROYAL VICTORIA MILITARY HOSPITAL
with thanks to Emily

White horses on a full tide,
blue-grey from shore to shore;
blown cloud, blown smoke
over the seaway –

where armies passed through,
and the wounded returned
out of battle.

       If we could see
the mass-grave of memories,
or see with the eyes
of one maimed man,
and smell blood
where the wind freshens,
this place would crush us.

But the space is open wide,
the day restored
to a child's eye, and where
men stared at ceilings
shocked with gunfire,
my daughter sits and writes.

Slowly I spell her words:

the shells that roll under the sea
the waves that roll and swerve
in the sun

AT THE RIVER-MOUTH

Always a working river,
bearing the weight of things:
boats beached on mud;
quays, wharves, docks,
an oil terminal.

Always a new world thrown up
on an old: shipyards
launching frigates over
prehistoric hunting ground,
a forest drowned in water mirroring
a forest on the shore.

★

Nothing at last, only
drops of the body
scattered and changed;
drops of moisture
on hulls and buoys.

★

Imagine that when at each instant
the river enters the sea,
nothing is lost,
but where the traveller
looking back through his past
sees the spire of St Michael's
sink vaguely behind a skyline
of cranes, the Itchen is one
from source to mouth, retaining
each grain, each wave
that forms it even as it breaks.

THE HEADLAND

1
Gold leaf, fire flakes
on silvery green
and a pool of ox-blood:

the sun
going down behind the Head
mixes with water and mud.

An old painter
who is nearly blind
sees in the foreground
the darkest dark.
But where, he asks,
is the lightest light?

One more bright day
afloat on darkness,
a picture scorched
with guttering flame.

2
At the harbour mouth
two men haul in a net,
which comes up slowly
with a catch of weed.
Nothing else until,
almost at the last,
a flash, a wild silver
thrashing – then
a blow from a stone,
once, twice, and the salmon
stiffens; drops
of moisture dry
on bloodstained scales.

177

Twenty pounds of meat
on a fishmonger's slab.

3
The place between the rivers
became Christ's Church,

because the Master had worked
with them, the masons said.
There was always one not
accounted for, and look!

The beam cut too short fits.

4
His people came
from fish-smelling streets,
from forest and saltings.

They brought a relic
of the cradle,
and heard the cry
that rocked the sea.

They sowed earth
from Gethsemane
on gravel and sand.

Across the harbour
the tower watched;
the Head's stronghold
eroded, and the rivers
brought down silt
and banked it up.

In the choir, carved wood
held a salmon leaping.
On the tower

178

a salmon weathervane
turned with the wind.

5

All is awash with colour.
Clouds slowly change shape
and shadow brushes the Head,
brightening gravel and sands,
rust-orange, yellow, black,
and pointing the doggers
of red ironstone jutting
from the cliff, like worn steps.
Not a lick of spray
for the channelled wrack,
only sun to dry it, sun
to wake the unseen tumult
between grains of sand . . .
The day blazes, burning
on the surface of millions
of years: fossil urchin
rubbed smooth and bone
harpoon, shark teeth
and tree trunk flattened in rock . . .
I fished from the groyne
as a boy, thinking the Head
would last for ever, but now
I know the groyne defends it,
and see in cliff-falls
and sandbars what thirty years
have wasted and made.
A butterfly flutters out to sea
and my eye follows, plunging
deep into burning blue.

6

I have come back
with redstart and wheatear,

a summer visitor, where
tribe followed tribe
for thousand of years.

On the Head a camp site
of reindeer-hunters
has fallen with the cliffs.

Flint blades struck
before the last Ice Age
mingle with beach drift.

To the west, a mirage
of towering hotels.
South, cloud shadow
dusts the dark blue sea.

In the harbour
aluminium wires
on masts and cross-beams
tinkle like sheepbells
in a rising wind.

7
The storm entered my mind
while I slept. I dreamed that water
shook our walls, and where
the priory stood a great river
with uprooted trees branched
like antlers plunged through the gap.
Only the Head remained,
gravel and windblown sand,
and beyond, a glint of towers.
Against the flood hook-lipped
broad shouldered salmon
thrust inland through blinding mud.

from
THEIR SILENCE A LANGUAGE
1993

~

Walked in rain from Barrow Moor toward Mark Ash and Bolderwood. ('Bolder' is Anglo-Saxon for house, but is this the same word as the name of the river, 'Boldre'?) Followed a small black stream, grass bright green around it; but difficult to get through the boggy low ground, and on the dry higher ground, bracken was more than head high.

Warm, slightly sweet smell of decaying leaves. Giant beech torso – the dead tree a new world: encrusted with several fungi, furred with moss, small trees and plants growing out of it – birch, rowan, bramble, fern – a home for insects, animals, birds; its roots like a large fragment of clay and pebble wall. Pieces of eggshell on the ground: so fragile among windfall sticks, under massive trees, but with their part in the immensely strong life continuing season after season. In a wood of old beeches the tree in its upward flight and cascade of branches is like a fountain beside the earth-bound oak.

Walking back, I felt a sudden brief fear when momentarily 'lost' – in fact, yards from the road, which was hidden by bracken.

STEPS

First is the feeling,
which I must trust, moving on –
cut into the void.

★

A passage opens –
that is where the drama is –
out of the covert.

★

183

To attain a truth,
work fearlessly, for ourselves.
We must break our taste.

★

You dance on the edge
of destruction, you dare see
what will come of it.

★

There is work to do
with fire – simplify the self –
charred and blackened form.

★

You finger the edges,
you execute the instant –
gallows-carpenter.

★

A rooted figure,
bound to earth but gesturing
at the open sky.

★

A human forest –
energy between figures,
linking them and us.

★

You shape the image:
it is a bridge we cross over
to meet in the world.

★

To know oneself shaped,
and work with knowledge of death –
that it may bear fruit.

★

Fern, gorse, pine, slow cloud
moving on – 'voice of the rhythm
which has created the world'.

★

One use of space is
for speaking across, another
to deepen silence.

∼

Walking all day in the Forest, I saw again how impossible it would be to convey a true impression of the ancient woods of oak and beech without showing that they are movements of light and shadow and air as much as countless tree-shapes; or rather that the natural 'pattern' continually changing around one comes from the interaction of forces and things which together make a world of the most delicate and subtle movements, and strong, deep-rooted forms. And this is only to sketch the surface, without regard to the interdependence of growth and decay, or of the many forms of life each with its own world in the world that human senses perceive; as for example insects under a scale of bark, a grey squirrel leaping from tree to tree, a woodpecker crossing a glade.

SO THE OLD SNAKE SHEDS ITS SKINS

Clash of flint with flint
that waves hurl against chalk

Risings, sinkings:
cycle on cycle

Fresh water, salt water,
brackish lagoon

Whirl and loop
of streaming gravel

Cloud on cloud of sediment

Yaldhurst: the tilled fields

~

Fallen cliffs, breakwaters – rows of stout posts standing out above the sea
– gravel, gorse to the very edge of the cliffs: these things move me
strongly.

They belong to love and friendship. Being with J at Hordle gave me the
beginnings of a poetry that was really mine. The posts are vaguely human
in shape and they stand for a massive effort that is only temporarily
effective and has to be renewed over and over again; and at the same time
they are completely non-human, insensate, and like a strange thing
emerging from the sea. They belong and do not belong, they become
part of the sea against which they are a defence, the waters they are meant
to break.

A sleeping painter and a sleeping sculptor come awake in my senses there.
When I come back the smell of the sea is on my hands.

BLACK ON GOLD

He dreams he is a painter standing
at his easel in an ill-lit attic painting
studies in black and gold.
A dead butterfly flutters in a breeze,
dances at the window in a filthy web.
Even when I was a boy (he thinks)

walking with a rod in April among the trees
I tasted filth. How free the mind?
A man – but what (he asks) is man? –
will do anything not to wake up.
He dreams he is a sculptor hacking
at the block that is himself.
It is black, black as rainwater
from the stump of the tree of knowledge.
Let me let in the gold (he weeps)
but the wood rots under his hand.
He dreams he is a poet writing
a poem about the shadow of a tree
leaning over water, where sunlight
touches the gravel bed with gold.
He is losing his bony grip,
the bank is eroding under him.
Wild bees swarm in the hollow of his skull.
He dreams he is a hunter chasing
the beasts that seek him.
On hands and knees, belly
dragging in mud, icy skin,
he follows where a black stream
runs through bracken into the wood
and a doe steps gracefully to the brink
and bends her neck and drinks.

~

I am conscious of being drawn to the same few things again and again,
and of seeking images of the life in them. Does this mean that I want to
relate to the things, instead of capturing them? Or to elements that
endure? Is kinship what I seek?

Perhaps there are many motives for an apparently simple act of naming
or image-making. And continuity is one of them. I have no sense that a
nostalgic haze colours the Forest as I look out on it from the train.
Nothing could be more distinct than the quality of dark or light, or the

187

wet bushes and trees, or Sway Tower as it disappears behind the ridge at
Marlpit Oak. I see what I have always known, and feel the things with a
child's touch, and because I am passing through.

FIRST TOUCH

A breath,
a touch of air
that feels so gentle,
so light,
on curve of wing and leaf.

A spider
poised on silk
which binds the furze.

Skaters
making circles,
dimpling the stream.

A fly
borne down
turning and turning.

Touch of the god
with broken hands
who rounds the globe of dew

OPENING

A butterfly alights
on a bramble flower

in a clearing in the woods,
and opens its wings wide,

trembling. It does not see me
apart from the trees, where

I stand watching silently
as it flies to another flower,

opens its wings wide,
and with a tremor, sips.

It is silver under wing
and above, bright orange,

almost gold, against
the leaves' darkening green.

Later I can learn the name
we have given it, but now

I only watch, tasting
the pleasure that it gives.

STEPPING IN

Unseen by the human eye,
hosts swarm, in the air,
in the earth, under bark.
Every dead thing renews
the fabric; oak walls grow.

Each footfall disturbs
a community. The wolf spider
hunts over leaf litter
which is his dancing floor.

This is the house
the sun builds, with air
and water and the green leaf.

Gods have thundered and passed on,
rustling the canopy.

CLEARING

'You are now your own carver, and must be
that which you shall have made of yourself.'
William Law

1
There are places in dreams that frighten me –
ruins at which I dare not look back.

Once, on the heath, a tower,
white as salt, with letters in gold,
cut high up on the face –
ancient laws, which I had no time to read.

I stood at the edge of the heath
with the tower behind me.
In front the ground sloped away,
and fell, and there was nothing.

It was where a dream ended;
where a dream had yet to begin.

2
Deep in the dark
an eye of white shows through.

I cut at brambles that clutch at me.
Holly slashes the back of my hand.
A branch like a tusk gores my side.

Stumbling on rotted wood,
breathing pollen and spores,
blindly I hack a way in.

Suddenly the dense underwood
springs apart, and for a moment
there is a clear space at the edge
where a figure stands –

a boy who whittles a stick,
a man who tests a blade against his skin,
a bone sculpture with blood running down –

But already the ground falls away,
and falls, and there is nothing.

~

Dark on the open plain, a holly 'hat'. (J. R. Wise, the historian of the
Forest, was certain that the word, which here replaces 'clump', origi-
nated from the high-crowned hats of the Puritans.) Dark green hollies,
their lichened trunks a lighter green – sombre, without berries. Nearby,
scattered silver bones of furze branches and stems. Nothing in the Forest
seems more enduring than holly and twisted furze.

A strong wind was blowing across the heath – we could hear it roaring
in a distant inclosure of pine trees. Over the pines, in good light, the view
leapt to a whaleback of Island downs. Grey cloud was blowing over, with
brighter, bluish-white depths where the sun almost broke through.
Shallow pools of water lay on the heath, and the soggy grass and moss
squeaked under our shoes. We crossed a broken concrete runway and
walked to Ocknell Pond. Here wind was brushing the surface violently;
it was just as if an invisible besom was sweeping across it, and with
sudden, more violent strokes, making the ripples fly in an arc, skittering
wildly, as fry scatter in panic before a pike.

The wartime airfields are haunting places. It is hard now to imagine any
of that – Hurricane squadrons, Mustangs, Wellingtons and Liberators,

gliders and practice parachute drops, all the makeshift life of encamped airmen and soldiers – where cattle and ponies feed among furze and the runways are minor roads. So much of that was, to me, a romance anyway, divorced from the emotions of the fighting men, set down in a place which must have meant to them something that it did not mean before the war and has not meant since.

YTENE

What knowledge hides
in the bones of gorse?
Their tough stems root
in the ashy soil of barrows.

I might be a Jute, weary
from the sea from which I turn,
the waste before me
the edge of a new world.

How close the knowledge is
which every thing conceals.

If I look hard, I must see it –
the ridges, the rolling waves
of moor grass, heather and ling
are a seaway with a destination.

I am thirsty from walking in the heat,
but when I have drunk,
and lie down on the grass,
it is what I don't know that parches me.
I am the waste the gorse roots in.

[*Ytene, an early name for the New Forest, has been said to mean either a furzy waste place, or the country of the Jutes.*]

'FROM'

He lifts up his shell
over his back. Does he know
what he is made of?

The shell feels like wings.
He tries to flap them. The wood
grows harder round him.

★

His body holds fast
to the earth. Yet he is, too,
a bow bent to shoot,

and the soul's arrow
drawn back, alive to his touch
in every feather.

★

His body's a bird
made from the bough it sings on.
His wings are the sky.

★

He hangs gracefully
like a hawk preying. Behind
him, poised, his shadow's

a man crucified.
Soon he will stoop and drop down,
blood spit on the earth.

★

Sometimes when earth opens
he grows into her.

193

He becomes sapwood.
His kin lodge under his ribs.
What is the thing men

boast of? His head shakes:
Man is branded on his brow.

★

He is always that
which he is about to be.
Now as he emerges

from the wood, he is
the tree walking, the passage
that will be his way.

Between earth and sky
his body stretches. He strides out,
and earth underfoot

thrusts and pulls. His flanks
are downland curved on the sky.
He is flame also –

wildwood flickering,
blazing through trunk and limb,
burning in the mind

of the maker carving
him, consuming dead wood,
shaping him anew.

[*'From' is a sculpture by Lee Grandjean*]

ELUSIVE SPIRIT

What is the quick, and where
is the spirit that eludes you?

There are rumours that seem
to speak of it here:
prickly fruit on a fallen tree –
dark butterfly that whirls up
fast and high, out of sight –
tap tap tap on dead bark,
the yaffle that flies away
crying his ancient laugh.

What stands revealed
for a moment, naked
as nails struck into wood?
All that hardens, dissolves,
dissolves and hardens.

Light stabs through clefts.
Hollows cup dark, in which creatures
that crawled from the sea bottom
millions of years ago
live on decay, enable life.

Even as you look, all
that appears solid transforms
root and branch.
                    Where
with a word you nailed down
that quick and elusive spirit
there is a flicker, a rustle, a sudden
sword dance of one bracken frond.
Dark whirls up with dead leaves
in a gust of sea wind, sun pours
where the trunks stand still.

DRUID SONG

Who keeps the vert and the venison?
Who calls the creatures into a circle?

The stag-headed one,
bearded with green leaves,
lies down with the tree that was windthrown
                              in its prime,
the lightning-shattered,
all the litter of the seasons.

These come again –
                              new wood, timber.

But Thor's tree is down,
the groves of the oakmen are felled.

There is no leaf, no twig
that does not grow upon the tree of life.

Where is the tree that will rise
to lift up the image of its maker?

STINKHORN

In one version the mother
mocks him for his pride:

Maker, Master of all things,
ramping where stags have rutted –
who laid the egg from which you burst?

Lord among creeping things,
your white flesh waxes and withers;
your stink attracts the flies.

Phallus Impudicus,
erect among leaf-litter:
what do you think you are –
Old Cock of the woods!

ALDER SONG

Alder carr
coppiced
by Avon Water –
as if to say
Water Water,
because one word
is not enough?

But these alders
long ago outlived
their human use,
and now grow simply
to be near water –
Water Water –
what word's enough?

LINES TO M

Crushed bracken fronds, where we lay.
(Remember the nightjar's churr.)

Dry river-bed through the woods,
Torrent of stone, tumbled and stilled.

~

The winter woods, you say, are a ruined cathedral. A downy feather falls between bare branches like a snowflake. Wood bleeds slowly from dead trees becoming earth. Suddenly, thousands of pigeons rise from the floor and fill the empty space with wild-beating, blue-white flashing wings.

ON THE ROAD THROUGH THE FOREST

All day all night
the carnival – pheasant

like an Indian head-dress
scattered on the road;

small birds tarred
and feathered; a fox

rubbed out, erased
to the last red hair

in grit, under our tyres;
soft thud of rabbits,

dancers with broken backs,
and in the woods,

in some nomansland
of the spirit, a smell

of petrol fumes; dead
embers of gypsy fires.

OAK SONG
for Carl Major

Oak
       at the back of the cold

after sedge and rush and Arctic birch
before the thief of fire
before the information of the axe

Noah's oak, laid
in drift gravel
with mammoth tusk

Black rings burnt in the soil

          ★

The lover of the tall stag
also appointed concerning the hares
that they should go free

The rich complained
the poor murmured

How sharply the man
in the covert sees
threatened with blinding

          ★

Skin for hide
skin for bark
nailed to the bloody tree

          ★

Oak
            for the makers of cruck and hull

Pickings of useful parts
knees and elbows
from doddards
though the body be decayed

'Caste acornes and ash keyes
into the straglinge and dispersed bushes:
which will grow up sheltered,
unto such perfection
as shall yelde times to come
good suplie of timber.'

                        ★

Saviour, protector, bearer
of the world's wealth –
stripped from the forest
that favourites crawled on,
leaf-rollers, baring the crowns

                        ★

Stacked, loaded
at Southampton Docks
for the trenches –
painted by an English Cubist
sharpening his vision

                        ~

At Queen Bower, following the stream through the woods, I saw the
heath blue as smoke in the sun.

Water dark green where deep and shaded; ochre, yellow, gold where the
sun came through, lighting sand or gravel shallows; a most beautiful
transparent green at the point of shelving and darkening. Pulse of

reflected water-light on tree trunks, and below, a procession of bubbles, and fragments of foam curling in an eddy, ceaseless corrugation of rapids, infinitely various shapes of branches and sky mirrored in still water, and the currents sinuous as eels. Sun splintered in countless glittering points, or its image held full and gleaming white, like a bright moon.

Returning to the stream from an excursion across an open space, I saw a herd of deer: white rumps and tall antlers moving peacefully between trees, not scenting me, perhaps, yet looking in my direction and apparently at me, without fear, but keeping half-hidden and well out of reach.

There if anywhere it's possible to see only what the Normans would have seen. What would a Saxon feel, even if about his lawful business, when caught up in the woods by a hunting party? Like a hare in hiding, perhaps, when huntsmen and hounds rush past on the heels of a fox.

THE CUT OF THE LIGHT

In hot sunlight
at the edge of the wood
a man's shadow cut
dark and sharp
against the path
beside the shadow
of a bracken frond
fine-boned
on mossed oak roots

Silently the marks that no man can read –
dapple, spot and stripe,
hieroglyphs on trunk and limb –
darken
        or vanish
              or are suddenly
a multitude of eyes, a blaze

The wood is a net, a wicker
of giant forms silently burning

Water is the walls
Water is the canopy
Water is the floor

Midsummer:
mast and tiny acorns form
berries redden by dark green leaves
silence deepens
                    to the human ear

A multitude of eyes
one blazing pupil

Shadow of a man
Shadow of a bracken frond

Now never now
the season the cycle
bark-year and wheat-year
(we say)
spring wood and summer wood
ring within ring

Beech fountains break
in spray of leaves
Oak walls made of sunlight
stream into the ground

~

The pattern again, like violent currents frozen in wood, or too slow for the eye to see, where growth has occurred and where it continues – the signature that all living things bear. Van Gogh's spirals, which some people see, and have to take care they are not driven mad.

RED KING'S DREAM

Surely it is nothing, like a song
about nothing. Yet it isn't the sun
that dyes the Lammas woods red
as I ride with my men through the trees.

Words echo among the boughs.
'You shall eat of me no more.'
What does it mean?

I hide what I hear with laughter,
with the gift of a bolt to Tirel.
I am the Red King;
I am the Conqueror's son;
my song's the twang of the arrow,
the rough, sweet voice of men.

Why should I fear nothing,
nothing at all, only
the blood-mist of a fading dream?

I was alone in a chapel,
deep in the woods;
it was richly adorned, as befits
a king and the son of a king.
I approved the purple tapestries
embroidered with legends.

They were old, older
than the Forest.
What did they mean?

Even as I looked they vanished;
the chapel was bare,
on the altar a stag,
which changed into a naked man.
'You shall eat of me no more.'

Whatever it means, let it be lost
in the flight of the arrow,
and the flight of the stag,
the great stag,
my beloved who dies for me,
soaking the earth with his blood.

COMPANY

'Mystery amid a great company of tree.'
(Heywood Sumner)

1
The wood is full of wounds:

limbs scattered, trunks
twisted and broken,
shells of sapwood standing
when the heart has gone.

And everywhere new growth
heals the wound, a seedling
needles the leaf-mould,
the dead stump bears a living shoot.

2
The wood is full of voices.

But where, where?
(the cuckoo calls),
where is the word that springs new?

3
Figures emerge from the trees,
stag-headed, wreathed with green leaves.

Darkness covers the site –
which light dissolves, opening
cavernous depth.

A sea wind gusts through the grove.

The space fills with sunlight
and shadows, whispering.
Where, where?
At the centre, the naked man,
wearing the holly crown.

In the trees
forked bodies twist and writhe.
Angels and beasts stare down.

Ghost haunts ghost
among the broken pillars,
under the tattered canopy.
The love song fades in the sigh of leaves.

A god with arms outstretched
bows down to the ground.

4
At the edge of the clearing
the great oaks stand,
massively bossed and knarred.

They do not hug the earth
but possess the sky.
Small oaks grow in their shade.

As we approach, they
seem to look at us –
their silence, a language.

WHERE THE GORSE FIRE WAS

A passage between walls
of flowering gorse
that reach high overhead.
Again the warm, spicy smell.
Indescribable.
Through the opening
twisted stems of blackened furze.

A path of white stones –
leached-white –
trodden by ponies
through dry, sandy soil.
On one side the gorse flowers.
On the other, charred limbs
writhe, like black flames.

PRESENT

The boy with a fishing rod
follows the river upstream
in April, among the windflowers.

The young man lies hidden
in a net of light and shadow,
naked, with his love.

The father walks under the trees
with his son,
who is laughing on his back.

And we call this *now*,
when the man stands still
in the woods in summer,
on leaves that we say are dead.

WINDLESS LEAF-FALL, WITH EMILY

We smell decay
and the earth-side of mosses.

Puffballs, acorns, mast,
chestnuts, fircones,
leached flints – already
they are half imaginary –

objects for her art class:
colours that tell a story,
shapes that make a world.

Oak leaves and beech leaves
fall around us,
spiralling down,
creeping through the air.

We find a small, clear pool
of water on a bed
of dead, golden-brown leaves.

And when we are lost
we meet an old man carrying
a full sack on his back
who shows us the way,

downhill, on a path
where we step carefully
over twisted roots;

but I see us dancing –
late brimstones turning
round and round, where
leaf falls lightly on leaf.

ALMOST NOTHING

She returns with the wind:
spirit-wolf,
grey between gorse.

Tongueless she howls with the gust,
moans in the hollow tree.
Formless she hunts for form.

What is too little to call to her?
A beetle-case sings of hope.
An empty shell harbours her desire.

She returns with the word
on the last human tongue –

almost nothing,
a body which the air
shapes from dust, blowing
under the wolf's-head tree.

THE NAKED MAN
*(With despair, as always
at the beginning)*

1
To begin, to begin again –

    Nothing
could be more dead than this tree.
It was once, they say, an oak,
and once, when the highway
crossed the rutted heath,
a gallows.

Now it stands
naked to winds from the sea,
stripped of the final skin,
bone of the bone.

A broken off trunk,
with concrete in empty sockets

                    I think it is like
an ancient being
held together and kept up
by a wooden scaffold.

2
Dead, the riven tree
rears up like a horse
with curving neck leaping
from the bracken –

a silver horse
among the brown ponies
grazing the open forest.

Dark blue clouds approach
threatening storm, gorse
and a few Scots pines stretch far
to the south.

The dead tree bends its silver neck.

3
To begin, to begin again
to make an opening –

What obstructs us but fear?
We must give what we have to give
body and soul.

You see the large, blind eyes.
He is there, the ancient wounded one
imprisoned at the core.

What emerges when you cut down
stands free of you,
and sets you free.

from
OUR LADY OF EUROPE
1997

1 *A TROY OF THE NORTH*

TO MIEKE

All day the stillness
of a storm that will not break.
After sudden violence of downpour,
thunderclap, the same clouds
shutting out the hills,
the sea a grey flagstone
at the town's back door.

The shadow of my hand
moved on the paper
heavily, marking
the space between us.
I sensed you far off,
in a deeper stillness.

If I were Dafydd
I would send my seagull
over the Welsh mountains,
across England and the North Sea.
Where you lie with eyes open
in the dark it would come to you,
bringing love and sleep.

BEGINNING AGAIN

Walking in the New Year,
blinded with splinters
of rain, almost blown
off the dyke into the sea,

there is no one behind us
in all the wide land
but a frantic scarecrow
dressed in a black suit
and running, running, running.

WILLEM BARENTS' LAST VOYAGE
(after Gerrit de Veer)

Past Fair Isle, we saw
a wondrous sign:
the sun, with a sun
on either hand, all
circled by a rainbow.

But after, sailing
the way of the north
we found Spitsbergen,
and crosses on a sea
of ice and darkness.

★

A bear, a white bear
on an island.
Blood in the sea,
and a bear swimming away
with an axe stuck in it.
We hacked its head to pieces,
we skinned it, and ate it,
but it didn't taste good.
We called our new land
      Bear Island.

★

Not a smell of Cathay,
but a sea spouting
whales & walruses –
possibilities
of commodity & utility
for those who further
and set forward ventures.

If we return
we will be a wonder –
men in caps of white fox fur
in rich Amsterdam.

★

Sun's absence, moon's light.
Our sand-clock's stuck to the floor
of our driftwood haven.
Bears claw at the roof,
skin sticks to iron.

We lie under snow and hear
ice crack,
out of the track of time.

★

He was our chief guide and only pilot
on whom we reposed our selves,
next under God.
'Gerrit,' he said, 'lift me up.
I must see the ice-cap again.'
He was looking at the map when
his eyes turned in his head and he died.

A TROY OF THE NORTH
for Alan Clodd

Seagulls mewing over reedy ditches,
but no one to sing the deeds, nothing

to tell the tale of a people
who did the work left undone
on the third day of Creation –

who shaped a mound of clay
on salt-marsh, and made
pasture at the brink of the sea.

Storm tides covered it,
over and over, spreading silt,
clogging ditches with corpses.
And what the sea did not drown
the Northmen burnt,
leaving blood-flecked foam
and homesteads blazing on the flood.

And again, over
and over again,
they took the measure
of water, and the weight
of clay, and raised the mound.

Nothing to tell
but a seawall far inland,
a dyke in the middle of fields,
cattle wading in summer pasture
and plots where hay lies
in windrows, like coarse yellow hair.

Bones dug into the earth,
site over site,

black earth and ashes
and the clay of makers and beasts.

And on the island raised above fields
that still smell of the sea,
the church of John the Baptist,
old red brick like dried blood
on a green hill, the tower
beside the body, a severed head.

CLOUDSCAPE
for Adam Hopkins

Wind-sculpted, white clouds
tower over us.

They are icebergs following
the route of the glaciers.

What are we doing standing
and looking up – tiny
on a flat ocean of clay –
if not to appreciate
what hills and mountains are?

A NEW LOVE POEM
for Mieke

A new earth
where not long ago was sea.

How do the moles know?
Already they snout in pale grey
sandy soil full of shells.

There is a poetry of dykes
against the sky —
a church spire — a windmill.
It is beautiful, and bodes peace.

Clods of earth cling to the flesh
of beets waiting in long mounds.
The unpicked cabbages
have a strangely expectant look.

Someone has lit a fire
in a corner of the day.

Red flames leap;
yellow reeds pierce the air.
But over all grey drifts down,
like silt clouding still water.

This is a poetry I know,
since you give it me.

IN PRAISE OF WINDMILLS

In the north the windmills stand
roundly on land and by water.

I take a leaf from the Windmill Psalter.
I name them, both the little and the great:

Young Hendrick and Four Winds,
Goliath and The Helper.

They have come far, but seem
to have grown where they are,
as native to the Netherlands
as sarsens to Salisbury Plain,
and as worthy of praise.

218

Yet Quixote was right;
they are monstrous.

                    If windmills
did not exist, Hieronymus
Bosch would have dreamt them.
They are living contraptions,
part insect and part bird;
mechanical creatures pondering
flight; earthbound,
flailing at heaven.

There are windmills in the mind,
alive to every breath of fear.

And things that hold firm:
cross-beams and quarter-bars,
crown-tree and king-post;
windmills that drive
and are driven, turning
indifferent winds to use.

They are labourers
at the brink of water;
old warhorses
that take the starving field.

No wonder people say,
The miller is a mighty man;
his hand spans earth and sky.
The great sails are dancing
but the painter holds them still.

The polder is a blank page
marked with a cross:
                    Goliath,
a little windmill but a giant

graced by need and by use,
solitary as a lighthouse
on a sea of blue clay,
in a land raised from the sea.

Over furrow and rhine,
I see the blade of a sail
shining, and think of voyages,
and stillness at the heart
of tumbling breakers
where the keel strikes home.

Behind the dyke the wind blasts
and the sea hungers.

Here the windmill stands
roundly by water and on land.

I take a leaf from the Windmill Psalter.
May the grace of the sails breathe in my song.

NOORDPOLDERZIJL

1
On one side of the dyke
a long, narrow road points
towards the far horizon.
Herons fish in ditches beside the road.
Ploughed fields flow away inland.

On the other side,
a long, narrow channel
pointing out to sea,
fishing boats moored
between green pastures.
Cows share the last grass with gulls.

2
A sluice, a handful
of red-brick houses –
but the place feels like the end
of a continent, somewhere
to sail from, over the rim.

What is it like to stay:
to live with the distances,
to lie down and wake at the level
of tides, listening, feeling
the pressures of the sea?

For generations, one family
has kept the sluice.

What keeps them, perhaps,
is *polderlust*:
a deep, slow rhythm
that ebbs and flows,
changing the sea to land,
and the land to sea,

and sometimes a quickness –
skim of the first swallow,
oystercatchers abandoning
the mud for the sky, piping,
dancing their mating dance
over the edge of the world.

STILL-LIFE

After long labour the place
is a patchwork of water and earth –
a broken mirror that shows the sky.

221

Slowly the brick walls crack,
the thatched, camel-backed houses
fall and are built again
on the same site, to the same design.

You see nothing of this,
drowsing on a wooden bridge
on an afternoon in late summer –
only rowan berries reddening
among leafy branches in peat-brown water.

The soil exudes a faint
hot-house smell and everything
is still, so still

that if a conker should fall
it would land with a thud
that rends walls, fissures the ground
and shakes the place to its foundations.

IN THE MARKET

I wake from a dream of death as falling endlessly through darkness.

Later, in the market, we stream along slowly with the crowd.

A girl chats to a customer while her fingers expertly fill and tie a bag.

Her skill gives me pleasure.

Men in white overalls shave slices off round, yellow cheeses and hand
them to us to taste.

How shapely the fruit and vegetables, how firmly they fill out their
skins.

Gradually I reinhabit my body.

Among all the fish with sightless eyes, the eels, in yellow plastic crates, are still alive.

They move their bodies against each other slowly, coiling and uncoiling.

I imagine a terrible gasping.

Something deep inside me, dull-flickering, dreams of breathing in the depths of the sea.

RIPOSTE TO MICHELANGELO

'. . . landscapes, and little figures
here and there.'

They have bricks to build with,
green pasture and the shade of trees.
Their bridges span still waters.

In the market, a man slices a fish
without pausing in his talk.
People handle fruit and cheeses.
Scales confirm measurements
made by hand and eye.

In the country,
thick, green water
mirrors creamy elder blossom
and bright blue flowers.
The sun winks on black pantiles.

God so made the world
according to the old masters –
broken men

who painted the substance
of things made whole
as it was in the first place.

In their landscape,
light is material;
it does not divide,
it does not dissolve,
but renders soul to body,
        body to soul.

Who is so little that he lacks
a place at the feast?

WESTERBORK
To the memory of Etty Hillesum

1
Our path lies along the Milky Way
and from planet to planet –

then out from the trees
and past the grey saucers
of the radio telescope.

Among toadstools, under oaks
loaded with acorns, we find
a solitary, white earth-star.

2
A few late foxgloves on a bank –
'sheltered'
I say, and the word echoes oddly.

Who can resist the ironies?
When will we recognise
that irony is not enough?

3
How understand the faces, Etty?
You looked at them
from behind a window
and were terrified.

You sank to your knees speaking
the words that reign over life
and bind you to these men
in the depths:

'And God made man after His likeness.'

Did you know they would murder you
and your kind?
That they would drive even the children
into hiding, and hunt them down.
And the patients. And the doctors.
All would be sent out on the Tuesday morning train.

4
The black train, which an artist
in the camp painted, looming.

But what amazes more
is his painting of a typical farm
and farmyard beyond the wire
as he saw them,
as we see them still.

5
At first there is little to show –
a few irregularities in the ground
of what might be a park.

Then we see what we expect:
a wooden guard-post,
preserved, or perhaps restored.

Below it, a short stretch
of the railway track reaches
from buffers towards the east;
broken off, twisted, the rusted iron
curves into the air.

6
And there, incised in stone,
a verse from Lamentations.

They hunt our steps, that
we cannot go in our squares . . .

You were a fountain of life.
Your love flowed into the world.

You looked for meaning
and found it even in the worst,
accepting 'all as one mighty whole'.

But the faces – how shall we accept
that you could see in them
instruments of destiny?

Whose faces, Etty?
What are they like?

7
Back from the universe,
back from the world,
back from the streets
of Amsterdam,
back from the houses,
back from the rooms
and the rooms behind the rooms,

226

you were driven, and driven in.

The space of your freedom
was at last a book, in which you wrote,
passionate to understand;

a mind behind the white face;
a card, thrown from the train window:
'we have left the camp singing.'

REIGERSBOS

Up in the wind, we hear a noise
of stick knocking on stick, a retching,
and looking up see long beaks,
long black hairs like antennae,
hunched figures, cloaked in grey feathers.

No longer the familiars
of ditch or dyke,
or bird flying east, flying west.
No more the hunter stick-still
at the lip of a rhine,
or the ancient one – pterodactyl
rising suddenly in evening light,
or statuesque on a rusting barge
moored under city walls.

Not now fishers
of common margins,
but strangers, rocking
on rafts of branches and twigs.

High in the wind, on tree crowns
echoing rounded, bright-edged cloud,
they clack their beaks
and look down at us with yellow eyes.

And what are we who gaze back,
wanderers over the brink of our own world
who have stumbled into theirs.

IN DRENTHE

for Rutger Kopland

1
A May morning
when oak buds prick into leaf
and the peewits tumble and cry.
Downriver, faintly, the cuckoo.

It is not what we expect
when a greenshank flying down
from a fence post lifts its wings
to reveal white feathers, and is
for that moment, an angel.

And surely the only one in this country
where the river flows rippling,
pulsing, and the sun kindles
the powdery sand, and beats
with white fire in the water.

It is more than we expect
and more and again more, when
the woods open on a meadow
yellow with dandelions
and you say, simply, 'It is a gift'.

2

Autumn, and the greeny, dark
river carries grass and leaves,
flowing slowly,
serpentine through meadows.

The glaciers crawled so far
and left the granite boulders
and the sandy ridge, the Dogsback.

And here the megaliths came
with the Neolithic track –
empty tombs, dark-gleaming.

In the blue sky, a daylight moon.
In the woods, toadstools –
red-capped, yellow, grey.
Stinkhorn, erect with shining skin
or half-eaten by flies.

So much to see, so much
to taste and touch.
But also a spirit that eludes –
in the light just so
on red leaf and yellow leaf
spinning, turning slowly,
as though each chooses to fall.

ISLAND CEMETERY

Within sound of the surf,
lapped in the sand of Grey Monk Island,
lie the dead of two wars and many nations.

From white headstones,
each at an angle, looking up,
the named and the nameless speak:

A. Wilson/Wireless op./Air Gunner/Age 18.
Master J.O. Roberts/S.S. *Firth Fisher.*
Sergeant Borret and Walter Weizel.
Ein Deutscher Soldat.
Inconnu. Mort Pour La France.
A Soldier of the Great War.
Known Unto God.

How tidily their graves are kept,
sheltered in a hollow among dunes,
each plot filled with cockle shells,
sea-washed, white and blue,
under the sign of the cross.

How orderly the lines,
how clean the words that speak to us
of the dead.
It is right to honour them.

We are stilled, hearing only
a faint bee-hum and the wash of the sea.
A salt air mingles with resin from Scots Pines
and a scent of roses.

Then we hear the birds –
oystercatchers, curlews, gulls –
all the different voices.
Shelduck fly over, long necks outstretched.
A harrier scours marsh beyond the dunes.

This is their world, and was
in the beginning – the same and again the same,
where they pipe and shrill and cry

whether monks keep the hours
or bunkers are built on the sand
and the dead wash ashore or drop from the sky,
mangled and burnt.

The sand does not quake; blood
does not cry out from the ground.
Only now we are not at ease
with a peace we have not won,
imagining an earth cleansed
of hatred of nations,
with a beauty that deceives the living
and simplifies the dead.

AFTER REMBRANDT: *THE ANATOMICAL LESSON*

It is one life
that shines in the dark eyes
of the surgeons who are bending
over the cadaver –
one life, unique in each.

The eyes of the dead man
are closed, his mouth
slightly open –
the mystery
has left this dead flesh

but shows in the eyes of the living,
in those who look down
at the exposed tendon,
the dissected arm,
or thoughtfully aside,

and in the face of the man
who looks at us,
wondering about himself,
mystified.

It is not yet only
a scientific question
that dawns in his dark eyes.

What is man? What am I
who am wonderfully
and fearfully made,
like this dead thing?

VINCENT

In the north
he goes among the people,
farmers, women who cut the peat.
He is a peasant-painter labouring
to paint peasants.

He is somewhere in the room
with them, struggling to paint
the hands they dig with,
and put in the dish, and share out their portion.

                    Darkness
comes out of the earth in the north.
It moulds the figures,
it shapes the farms.
This is the good soil of Holland,
the soil the poor live on.
It means hardship, not misery,
not the dry, dusty wind of the Borinage.
The cold wall of the church

chills him to the spine,
he is a servant
of the man-forsaken god,
a light-bringer
who loves the dark.

Earth is new in the south – bright yellow,
vermilion, burgundy, violet,
sky blue, bright green.
Earth melts, burns with a flame
that does not destroy but restores.
This is the force life lives by,
the force he seeks to enter.

The sun roars in the harvest field.
He holds the yellow note,
the black cypress is a vortex
and the heavens rain down fire.

Gauguin paints him painting sunflowers,
in which he sees himself 'gone mad'.

He paints irises in the asylum garden,
tongues wagging, the silence
loud with shouts and screams.

He has gone out of hearing,
he is somewhere deep in the fields,

a stranger in a foreign land.

ROTTERDAM: ZADKINE'S *DE VERWOESTE STAD*

1
Bronze Atlas, with a mortal wound.

But still powerful:
a contorted giant, hands raised,
reeling in agony. Not defeated.

He is the city that will live again
when a bird builds its nest in the place
of his burnt-out heart.

2
When he was a boy
our friend saw the sculpture
lying in pieces, waiting
to be assembled and raised.

Now he often leaves his office
during the day, and walks on the waterfront
watching the ships.

He thinks of his father and grandfather,
of the river that will go on
when he is dead,
and he feels glad to be
'a minor part of it, but a part'.

Does he know how much rests upon him?

How lightly he shoulders this world.

DREAMING OF EUROPE: A COLLAGE

How good our nights and days
of making love on the roof garden
among spires and towers
lifted up on a level with clock faces
we did not see

★

THIS COULD BE A PLACE OF HISTORICAL IMPORTANCE

He has a taste for ambiguity
which he inscribes in stone paving
in front of the cathedral:

1. Something happened here you should know about.
Do not spit or dance on the spot.
Cover your head.

2. It is just possible that something important might happen here.

3. Think about it.
You could change the world.

★

It is certain that when she was a little girl
the big, black thing frightened her.

Now we are overawed,
the blackened stone spires
look down on us.

Inside, the upsurge of power,
graceful, light.

It is invested with a presence:
the after-image of bomb damage.

How many did it save?

★

It is impossible to leave the parapets of Europe.
You cannot abandon the fathers,
they come after you with retorts and muskets,
scissors and rolls of cloth.

You may trek across deserts
or sail over the rim of the world,
but the germ is in you.

Even in dreams
columns of water thunder to the ground,
cities are swept away.

Or a white wolf sits in a walnut tree
outside the window, looking in.

★

I believe in the head of Hans Arp.

It is a potato or an apple
or some good fruit he grew
from the tree of his imagination.

★

We learn to walk with the Christ child
on a walking-frame.

With a windmill, he teaches us to play.

He opens his arms with the generosity
of a drunkard.

236

Magnified in the minds of men
he becomes a demon who drinks our blood.

★

I believe in Hans Arp and Sophie Taeuber
and the visitation of angels.

Angels are no economists.
Magnificently
they squander the light.

★

Does the wood see, does the field?

It is not after all the worst thought
that no one watches, spying
into every shell-hole and crack.

★

Longing is the road they travel.

Every one a stranger
searching for the lost home.

It is not here, not there.

★

After they were driven out
they sought shelter in a cave
and wore garments which they wove
from animal skins.

It was the best time, they would learn to say.

2 WRITTEN IN CLAY

FENRIR

The terror slips from its dream image
along forest tracks and pathways of the mind,
and emerges scrawny,
exhausted by a long winter,
sniffing at the town garbage dump.

For now, the sun may complete
its nuclear explosions with impunity
out of the reach of slackened jaws.

ON A PORTRAIT OF EDITH SÖDERGRAN AS A CHILD

Nothing can stop it happening, Princess,
for already with your wondering
and frightened eyes you have chosen –
flash of gunfire over the frontier,
black flags at the sanatorium window:
a conscious dying – into life
that is shaped anew?
No one will prevent you, child,
from flying to the rooftops,
alone and eaglehearted – to look out,
to pluck the strings of a lyre
that stretch from roots of forest trees
to stars that take their fire
from the furnace burning in you –
pale and deep-sea creature,
magic child, woman whom no one knows.
Nothing will abort the birth
of a man-god, poet, or stifle song
within you, which you feed with blood.

VERDUN

in memory of Franz Marc

Thistles, poppies, blue cranesbill
by a dusty road.
In front, under the cloud stack
of an August sky,
                    the chalk ridge.

Trees, flowers, the earth
all showed me every year
more and more of their deformity.

★

On a bluff a machine-gun post,
an iron mask with two eye-holes,
looks down on new growth.

Inside, the remains of a gun,
rusted and twisted.

The mask that blinded
has survived the face. It overlooks
slopes with harebells and young pines.

In spiritual matters new ideas
kill better than steel.

★

Deer feel the world as deer,
but whose landscape is this?

All things, all creatures
are on fire. *All being*
is flaming suffering.

239

Under pine needles, the earth
that bled for purity
is matter,

        pulped and shattered.

I dream of a new Europe

★

EN MEMOIRE DE FLEURY DEVANT DOUAMONT
She is Our Lady of Europe,
her chapel stands on rubble
under pines, on blasted,
cratered ground.

Where the village was
the woods are dark and still
but the chapel in a glade
is filled with sunlight.

A white butterfly wanders in
and flutters outside the porch.

★

New Year 1916. *The world
is richer by the bloodiest war
of its many-thousand-year history.*

And all for nothing.

[*The words in italics quote, or adapt, translations of Franz Marc's words.*]

TOWARDS ARRAS

From Picardy and the land of the Somme
the late summer sky had lowered,
become a roof of dark blue cloud.

And it broke in downpour, shattering
on roadside memorials and regiments of graves,
smoking across the fields,
the mounds and ditches, that already,
after seventy years, look prehistoric.
And as we drove towards Arras,
slowly, against the pounding
and blinding cloudburst,
I thought of Edward Thomas
and how he would have loved
the violence of this passing storm.

THE STONES OF BRITTANY

Most of them dwarf us

                        the menhir
shaped like a giant phallus
that has fallen and broken

                        the passage,
symbols carved in granite,
a fine axe
which might also be a plough
furrowing the stone

                        the alignments
which could swallow a multitude

the one I return to
is a broken circle,
stones on the shore
of an island of megaliths,
stones in the water
gulls and cormorants
perched on their heads,

which the tide covers
and withdraws to reveal
again
                    the circle

wave-shaped curves of the beach,
the curves of the windrows
of dark brown wrack,
earth wheeling
                    the turning sky

HIERATIC HEAD OF EZRA POUND

Scholars will speak of vision,
even, without irony, 'the final vision'.

The mind of Europe
founders among its ruins.

Words must fail.

The man looks up. The light of the stockade
glares in his eyes.
He is guarded, and displayed.

There is no shadow for him here,
unless it is memory
peopled with shades:

                    Gaudier
in his studio under the railway arch,
a man of the renaissance,
the air between them alive with ideas.
They dispose of an age of statues,
a trash of books.
The poet is quick to give.

242

The sculptor works on the marble,
winning every inch
'at the point of the chisel'.

Naturally, the sculpture
will survive the carver,
and outlast the model.
It will gaze back down the century,
over the work of other men of order
whose material is flesh and blood and bone.

The Head looks impassively over the ruins.
The poet looks out
towards the mountain, beyond the Pisan cage.

TWO FIGURES FROM CATALONIA

1
They called him Bes, he was a god
brought over by the Phoenicians.
A gross, flabby figure,
a cross between a wrestler
and a dissolute Buddha
with a worn, distorted face.

          We can't tell
what he meant once,
but he retains some power
          he makes us smile.

2
She too is time-worn
but her beauty is palpable,
desirable.
         It is not
that she might have risen from the sea

yesterday
with the mucous glisten of birth
still wet on her skin.
                      She belongs
among the dusty paths, stone walls,
holes in the ground
and to the hot sun, and dark
eternal flames of cypresses.
      She is Aphrodite
in whose beauty
desire calls to desire
making, unmaking, the bonds of time.

ODE TO ANTONIO GAUDÍ

When I first saw
the façade of the Nativity
I laughed, and wanted to cry
and the imp in me itched to say
to the imp in him, 'So this
is what can happen
when parents let little boys
play with sand!'

But it was not like the work
of that other devout man,
Gerald of Wales,
who built cathedrals
in the sand at Tenby,
and grew up to be a bishop.

This was about play
more than power,
and more than both,
and as well as both,
it was about wonder,

244

Gaudí's, and the wonder
of the people (myself
among them) who stood
amused, intrigued,
amazed, and first and most
of all, wondering.

This was about being a man
who was a great artist
and a child, who made
a thing that stands, and flows,
and seems to melt and run
and drip, like water
or forms that grow in water
and embody its rhythms
and its shapes.

The work of a man
who knew the Adoration
of the Serpent and the Beast;
who had seen angels riding
the winds on wineskins;
St Michael with wings
made of peacock feathers,
slaying a monster that lies
on its back exposing
an orange belly, like a newt's.
This man's familiar was
John the Baptist, wide-eyed,
brown-bearded, standing
in a desert of cacti
that leap about him like green flames.

And their makers, the makers
of these images, were his people,
the people he belonged to,
with whom, at another time,

he had embroidered
the Tapestry of Creation
using the umbrella pines,
the Catalan soil and fields
for materials and tools.

Gaudí of Barcelona,
the city that gave him freedom
to embody such a vision
and most deserves his blessing.

He died, the great work
unfinished,
and because of that
more natural, more
a place to play in,
and laugh and cry
and wonder at the maker,
man-child, and his praise
in the body of Creation
that begins and has no end.

THE MOTHER OF LAUSSEL

You may know her by the rock
she is made of, and the scars
of the ice.

She is the one who nurtured the bison,
and starved it,
and holds aloft its horn,
which is also her symbol,
the crescent moon.

She is without a face.
Is she, then, Goddess of Love?

Examine the deep breasts,
the bulging thighs,
the curve of her belly.
With her free hand
she points down, between her legs.

She stands at the cave-mouth
and is herself the cave.
This is the birthplace
of the rock rose and the sabre-tooth.

You will recognise her
by a touch, when, for the last time,
you kiss the cold brow-bone
of the woman who bore you.

3 CROSSWAYS

TEL GEZER

And Solomon built Gezer.

*How simple the words that have only
one meaning – blood.*

1
I wanted to ask you, Shimshon,
after that day when we worked together
in the fields, breaking the stony soil
and planting young olive trees,
when blisters wept on my hands
and the sunflowers in the heat
seemed also to turn their faces
to talk to each other, as you to me.
That day, Shimshon, black Hebrew,

soldier and lover of trees,
just man, but fierce and strong
in defence of your people, you
told me the history under our feet,
in the kibbutz and the Tel rising
above us as we worked, hacking out
thistles and tough-rooted fennel,
making room for the young olives.
And at night, as I lay in bed
with aching body, between sleep
and waking, images blazed,
or fell dully like drops of blood,
and voices crossed in my head.
My friend, I wanted to ask you
the meaning of the words.

2
A language of soil,
cracked and brown,
with a look of old parchment.
Fields of sunflowers.
Then pine trees and limestone boulders
as the hill climbs.
A path to tread carefully,
dry and pitted,
where red ants swarm
carrying seed-heads.
Caves. A prickly pear cactus.
Concrete floors hidden in grass,
a spent cartridge among stones.

In the heat, the Tel is alive
with insects and birds. A tortoise
rustles dead thistles, regards
the intruder with a black eye.
On the great mound, a row

of standing stones. And five storks,
which fly off under a moon
like a partly blown dandelion clock.

Has history burnt out history
in this place, and left nothing?

Image throws down image,
word shatters word
in the silence.

The cracked earth gapes
with dusty mouths.

Land in the heart
of an Arab poet in Paris,
who looks through boulevards
at a stone village
with vineyards and olives.

Land in the heart
of a Jew staring
through the walls of Europe
at bare, waiting earth,
sun like honey on the stone.

3
From a deep cleft on the Tel,
a hawk flies out of the ground
and sheers off, circling, wind-ruffled.
Grassblades quiver under it.
And here the hawk has preyed since
before Pharaoh destroyed Gezer
and Solomon rebuilt it of mud
and stone, or the Assyrians
perfected the art of exile; since

long before the kibbutz formed
a small, green pool below,
in the dustbowl of stony hills.

Tel Gezer: where the road
from Egypt to Syria
crosses the road from Jaffa
to Amman, with the Mediterranean
a long, bright sliver in the west.
Mount of Temptation for a people
with everything to lose,
and a people with nothing;
who look down on the valley of Aijalon
where the moon stood still,
and Latrun, the House of the Good Thief,
and over the hard hills of Judea
towards Emmaus on the road to Jerusalem.
Each name in this place is a sound
of approaching thunder – it would hollow
the skull with a blast of fire
to see what it means.

Tel Gezer at the crossways:
destination of roads
from Warsaw and Buchenwald;
exodus of Arabs from Abu-Shusha
and El-Biryeh and El-Kubab,
on the road to refugee camps,
kicking up the dust of Palestine.

4
Pharaoh has gone up and taken Gezer
and burnt it with fire.
He has overrun the perimeter
and slain the Canaanites.
Nomad falls on nomad
for the olives and vineyards

and stony ridges, for a dream
that flows with the hills
and settles in green valleys –
that the wolf lie down with the lamb
and a little child lead them.

Captives scratch their hatred on the rocks.
A curse on Simeon, may fire descend
from heaven and devour his house.
A curse on the Christians.
A curse on Saladin and the heathen.

A curse on the Jews –
our hills speak it, and the mouths
of dynamited wells,
the rock speaks for us,
and the silence and the red wind
that blows from the desert
and every crack in the soil.
There is no bare earth –
each stone has sucked up blood
and memory inscribes the dust.

Our memory – and now we are afraid
to appear in our fields.
Let the Jews seek their friend
where he lies sightless on the Tel
and a tortoise eyes him curiously.

And Yusif lies buried
in the rubble of his home.

5
The young orchard demands our care.
We go out with rifles, one eye
on the work, the other on the rocks.

What calls?
A bee-eater, brilliant blue and green.
At a touch each rock may stun and blind.

Will the golden fields wait in vain
for the combines?
Will Arab hatred silence the harvest?
We have put sweat into this land.
We had nothing – the very name
of Man cut from our foreheads.
And now hold a home, a camp
among enemies, a foundation stone
of the State.

Summer comes, fruit ripens, swallows
high in the blue are small as bees.
An army comes out of the hills.

They cross the perimeter with tanks,
circling, driving us in.
First the stable is hit, then
the fuel-tank; hay-sheds blaze
and the air is thick with smoke
and stench. What does it mean?
You know the bodies are comrades
you won't see any more, and no one
will replace you if you fall.

At night we counter-attack: no one,
only a few Arabs looting the rubble,
scattering feathers from quilts
and pillows to the wind.
They melt away into the orchard
and through their empty village streets.
They vanish into the hills.

6

A pine marten moves sinuously,
with alert head, over the grass
and by the cypresses, past
the Hebrew graves.
At the foot of the Tel, a wall of names –
people from ghetto and death-camp
who came here to make a home
from bare earth, and died together
on a day in June when the harvest
was waiting in the fields. And now,
at the start of a new day, Shimshon
drives out a tractor, and Jewish children
crowd round him, their hero and friend.
No snipers, no ambush today
among the huge limestone boulders
and fortified caves. No detail
sent to eliminate neighbours.
A bee-eater calls, alighting on
Solomon's mud wall, and lizards,
dragon-headed, look over the edge
at red ants swarming on the path
and rusted tank tracks lying in a tangle
of herbs and passion flowers and barbed wire.
Now it is a place of swallowtails,
of hawk and eagle, and the storks
on their flight from Africa to the Elbe.

From the kibbutz and Hebrew cemetery
the path climbs to Abu-Shusha –
but there is nothing left, only
potsherds and bits of white mosaic
sprinkled with dust.
There are moshaves on the sites
of El-Biryeh and El-Kubab.
Opposite the Tel, looking down

to Aijalon and Latrun and the road
to Jerusalem, a new village,
and Arabs working in a vineyard.

Below the site of the orchard,
where the border used to run,
sunflowers shimmer in the heat.
They pulsate, full-faced, or hang
dried heads, heavy with seed.
Bees yellow with pollen climb out
and lumber away through the air.
The flowers seem to dance when
the wind stirs, then turn to each other
in a golden, silent conversation.

The young olives stand in the sun.

Will they grow thick with fruit?

Who will harvest them?

JERICHO

1
Oasis of flowers and fruit,
green in the wilderness:

hibiscus and bougainvillaea
among date-palms, red
acacia sheltering houses,
lemons and oranges in the streets.

No reason here for a man
to renounce the world,
who builds a winter palace

by the Mountain of Temptation,
with all good things that water
and wealth provide –

a dancing floor, courtyards
and shady chambers, a mosaic
cool under his feet –
the Tree of Life,
full of leaves and heavy with fruit,
flanked by a lion
leaping on a gazelle.

2
Hard and dry under the sun,
Old Jericho is a stairway
into the ground, down through
mud-brick and beaten clay,
walls tumbled on walls,
tower on tower, down
through debris choking the way –
and no moist tongue, nothing
but a clay tablet to speak
for thousands of years.

At the bottom of it all,
the floor on which hunters
made a camp and raised a shrine
by a spring watering the desert.

3
That none should be lost –

all things speak against it:
the sandgrains that want
only to be forgotten,
buried in the sandhills;
the water that flows,

moulding all to its nature;
the powers that go down
stroke on stroke, butchering
or being butchered
for Mammon or for God.

He who knows their names
and those of their children
and of their families, may he
inscribe them in the book of life.

BETHLEHEM

Over all, suddenly, with a crash
that sends sheep scrabbling
at stone walls or squirming in the dust,
a jet fighter crosses the target area.

Over David's fields and the trunks
of felled olive trees, two thousand
years of life compacted, swirling
in the wood. Over stony fields,
hard, white hills and Herod's
mountain tomb crowning the wilderness.

All look up blindly –
women from weeping at Rachel's Tomb,
soldiers at roof-top gunposts,
Arabs selling fruit in Manger Square
or at lathes turning out holy figures,
a tourist enjoying the ironies,
who remembers another place:
starlight on the home fields,
voices drawing closer from door to door

O little town

★

They will sing a new song
descending from the fields
of galactic dust,
from the black cold
by the blaze of nuclear suns.

They will come down
out of the nebulous dark
to the ruined stable,
gas shell and shattered atom
lighting the night they blindly stare at

★

And so we enter
under an old doorway
made to keep out animals,
and descend through histories:

between pillars stained brown
as old canvases, under
ikons and a brass hanging lamp
balancing a tzar's crown,
past symbols, past stonework
of Crusaders, Armenians, Greeks.

Under the gaze of Elijah
over the long falls of his beard
we come to the mosaic floor
and the floor below the floors,
down to the simple place
all has been built to protect,
or bury . . .

when, suddenly, with a crash
that shakes the walls,
a jet fighter crosses the hills

and we stand with candles
shaking in our hands

★

Lantern light on faces
under the shadowy cross-beams.

So the scene is set:

Mary wrapped in a night-sky cloak.
Ox and ass, big-eyed, nuzzling
into the cradle.
Joseph leans head on hand, resigned
to what he loves but does not understand.

★

A smouldering warmth,
fire in the dead of the year,
a red glow at the heart
of black cold, and starlight
falling through the broken roof,
a smell of hay,

the child's cry among the farthest stars

WALKING TO CAPERNAUM

1
Such violence struck here –
a new thing, a word with power:

And thou, Capernaum,
which art exalted unto heaven,
shalt be brought down to hell.

A gentler word
where the sea laps the shore:
the damsel is not dead, but sleepeth.

2
What I feel most is the heat,
and sick at the unreality
of bad art:

a sloppy English poem
which someone has fixed on a wall
at the site of the miracle
of loaves and fishes;

new stained glass daubing
the interior of the chapel built
over the rock where Christ
is said to have said to Peter . . .

Compared to these,
I could love the wooden donkeys
and camels and holy families
from the factory at Bethlehem.

Unreal, in a sweat of heat
and bad blood, I dip
my seamy face in the water.

It tastes of salt, and is
a dull silvery blue
on a day of desert cloud.

A crane – not, thank God,
a symbol – but a white crane,
with long, wispy hairs at the back
of its neck, stands
fishing in the shallows.
A black lizard looks at me
over the edge of a black stone.

3

On the road between
orchards and tomato fields;
in the dust thrown up
by tourist coaches;
between the columns
and among pine needles lying
on the ruins of Peter's house,
I try to imagine them:

The girl waking surprised
with hunger in her eyes;
the woman cured by a touch;
that loud cry, the man
on the floor of the synagogue –
torn and empty, but clean.

What had he seen? What thing
had cried with his voice?

And the fishermen
as they put out –
from this moment, no
denial will swerve their aim.

The port they left behind
is a heap of blackened stone.

4

It is evening, and very still;
heavy cloud, the colour
of smouldering ash,
obscures a misshapen moon.
Tiny fish swarm blackly
on the surface, nudging
crusts from our seafront café,

Suddenly, the wind rises. Trees
sway and open, lights go out
and napkins soar into the air;
waiters leap to catch bottles
and glasses blown off the tables.
A cloud swirls through the streets
and covers our plates with sand.
At once the sea heaves up
a huge, slippery shoulder
against the wall.

In the sudden violence
I see them for the first time:
the small port waiting, still
waiting – nets spread on the wall,
barrels of salt fish on the quay –
and the men who will not return,
but are borne up at a word
as their ship drives through the storm.

4 MOTHERLAND

HOMER DICTATING
for Gerard Casey

It is the body that speaks
and what it speaks of is the man
and his suffering, his thought,
the vision he sees in his blindness.

His hands speak,
and his mouth speaks more than words,
and his whole body,
an old man's but still powerful.

In the depths behind his eyes
warriors boast on the windy field,
Odysseus adventures on the seas,
among magical and dangerous islands,
and strains his eyes against the light
and sting of spray to catch a wisp of smoke
far off, rising from the hearth-fires of Ithaca.

Rembrandt's Homer is a man,
but the light of the sacred
is upon him –
a pale watery gold
falling across his shoulders and his face.
But it does not shine from afar,
from another world.
The sacred is part of him,
dwelling in light and shadow,
and his body is the landscape of his soul.

For the painter has taken clay in his hands,
common clay,
and shaped from it the image, God-given,
which he knew in his own world,
among merchants and soldiers,
Rabbis and adventurers,
the grand and the poor of Leiden
and Amsterdam, and knew
most intimately in his own flesh,
in the imagination that is breath and blood and spirit.

With this he saw, and humbled his seeing
to know the vision of the blind,
of Homer dictating,
with sightless eyes,
the seer of men and women and gods.

PANAGIA KARA

Our Lady the Virgin,
white-washed among cypresses,
where the shadows bear fruit
and the familiar becomes strange:

    a rich darkness,
a painted cave,
but not where Zeus was born,
or Kronos slobbered,
swallowing a swaddled stone.
Serene, accepting, this Christ
is stronger than the savage gods.

Cool, pictured shadows –
green & red, orange & brown –
show the Nativity. Herod's massacre.
Grapes and lemons grow, birds sing,
on branches of Paradise.

On the table of the Last Supper
a wonderful fish –
surely a red mullet –
looks at us, and winks.

PALIKARE

Later we will see him –
      his lean, strong, stone-carved face –
but today we see,
on the ascent,
        hooded crows
and what might be eagles,
three big birds, just glimpsed,
circling a crag.
        There are lemons,
oranges, silver-leaved olives,
white anemones;
        even here,
in mist on the heights,
           the horn of plenty.
But we will not remember them
as we remember the skulls,
the glass cases
        filled with skulls.

      It is Easter,
the church is prepared
        with lilies,

it is time to think of courage
                              and death.
This is the place.

I can hardly credit it,
even here, in a country
where courage is common as rock,
and grows from it
                              hard face
to hard face.

                              To destroy
your people, your kind –
men, women, children –
                              and destroy
the enemy, who otherwise
will defeat you
                              and take all you have.

To die together
in one blast,
                              friend, enemy,
stripped of the names,
lying together,
                              skulls
that are indistinguishable
one from another, but not to you
                              who know them
absolutely
                    at the last moment
that never ends,
                              each
a living soul.

You recognise them,
                              every one.
You bring them, shepherd

265

to the pastures,
                    the green fields
of the dead.

I have heard of courage, Palikare,
but it would be a lie
to say I understand.

Later I will see you,
                    your lean, strong face
carved in stone.

EUROPA
for Lindsay and Phoebe Clare Clarke

The sun stands naked
out of the shade, in a space
of poppies and fig-trees,
                    an empty space
where Greeks and Romans built their worlds.

                    Over all
the breath of the bull-god,
the sear of lightning that burned
a blackness into the light.

What havoc it caused –
columns, sarcophagi,
a headless female statue,
the dome of St Titus,
                    emptied,
filled with flutterings
of sparrows.
                    And a side chapel
where the faithful and the sick
bring medicine bottles,

prayers for healing,
ikons of the Virgin;
where I placed a bunch of grass
in memory of a dead poet, a woman
who knew the value of such things.

*

What did he know
the Philosopher of Gortyn?

Here he is a peripatetic
among Pans and Roman nobles,
a man with a fine beard
and sandalled feet,
a museum piece
that is almost whole.

What idea? What salve
for the wound between us,
the emptiness, worlds
vanished into the ground?

*

Once, they say,
Earth was a giant pithos
pouring out oil and wine
embracing the dead.
                    No war troubled
the forests and mountains
or bloodied the inshore water.

Then the air darkened
with the flight of the god.
She clung unwillingly to his back,
fingers wound tight among curls,
that moments before had plucked flowers
where she walked by the shore.

And so, with the waves
still swimming in her eyes,
she was laid down and the bull
hung over her, a cloudy mass,
            and bore her down.

It was here, under the plane tree,
where the stream runs
and the water is living,
            never so living,
under the naked sun.

EARTH SONG CYCLE

Women dancing in a field of poppies

Slowly at first they measure
their steps as the sun strengthens,
the poppies flame redder,
the sea-blue deepens, and they,
women in white, loose-limbed,
flowing, circle hand in hand,
turn faster, and faster,
leap and fly till their feet
are birds, white birds, skimming.
And round they go, wing to wing,
as the field revolves and the sea,
and earth veils and unveils, ·
white and blue, under their heels,
which skim and pause and come to rest
while round and round them turns
the scarlet field,
            and O the earth.

She descends into the dark

For now she knows nothing
but terror, rage.
                    And what she throws off
is the scent of it, the reach
of the stamens that beckoned,
the face of the flower
that drew her in, and closed,
as a sundew swallows a fly.

                    Beyond this,
the meadow spins in her mind.
She feels on her hands the hands
of her friends, gripping,
torn away.
                    It is a lost world
she sees in the dark
and nothing more, not the god
whose sweat she smells
and breath she feels on her face
as he drives her down.

                    Later she will see,
but now there is only his breath
mixed with the reek of horses,
the smell of roots
and engulfing earth.

How can she know what visions
will be born of her story,
or even if it is true?
There is, perhaps, no power
but hers, no god to command.

This is not the moment to see,
nor the moment of those

who will follow, seeking her
under the ground.
                How many will come
as the light fails, or the glare
extinguishes sight.
                How many
will plead with her
for annihilation
or beg to return.
                Only now
the dark has taken her
and she has left, to her friends
reeling apart in the meadow,
and her mother, listening
to the echo,
                only a cry.

And every cleft is mute

A cry echoes among the mountains.

                        Somewhere
the earth has opened. Where?
Where is her daughter?

She searches and searches
but finds no sign.

Who cares? Not the god
who leaps and dives and plunges
to death in ecstasy
and forms again among the foam.

Not the stones she kicks over,
or the cuttle-bones
or globs of tar.

Not the roots she finds
sodden with salt –
            images
that would bewitch her,
grotesques
with human form.

Are these, maybe, a sign?
She calls again
and no one answers.

The sea changes.
It is clouded glass,
into which she looks, and sees
nothing.

No one. Every cleft
is closed against her call.
She sets her bleeding feet
on shells, weed, foam.

Turning over, the waves
are cavernous,
smooth for an instant
and full of sand.
            Light rides in
on crest and underlip.

The day will be immaculate,
the night perfect, that sees
her torch wandering in blackness
like a moon.

She hides her golden hair

Let him bellow,
          the thunderer
wrapped in cloud,
for this, she says,
is only the beginning.

          Birds
returning to her without a message
drop dead from the sky,
snail shells bleach in heaps
spiralling down to dust,
snake and green lizard
crawl into holes to die.

And she hides her hair
in a hood.
          As a stormcloud
falls on the harvest,
blackness blots out the gold.

          She walks alone
among her people, searching
their sightless eyes
for a sign.
          No one answers
when she calls and calls.

Men break picks on the fields,
oxen strain to shift the plough,
seeds fall on soil turned to stone.

          She will waste all
as she is wasted,
calling and calling.

Ovens and storage bins,
the giant pithoi
that poured out bounty,
all their round bellies
hold emptiness and mould.

And this, she says,
is only the beginning.

        Afterwards
the fall of ash,
seas white with corpses,
no swellings on earth
but the bloated dead.

        Let him look down
on his handiwork,
           thunderer,
father of desolation.

        Who will survive
to make an offering
or give him thanks,
when she, who brings
all things in their seasons,
provides nothing,
and no one but the dead?

A hymn to Demeter

Pardon us
that we will
our end & forgive

the poet
his ambition
to stand alone

273

on a high peak
surveying
the waste.

Take the map
from our hands
which we take
for the world

& let us be
where earth
and waters meet

& make, for you,
a song.

'Christ is risen!'

Again the priest
has cried aloud
in a joyful voice
to the people
who move off together
carrying candles,
a procession
of white moons
threading the dark.

Once more a cry
sounds where a cry
has echoed
over corn field
and olive grove
across thousands
of years. Again
the cave stands open
and the faithful see.

Written in clay

What could he do, the swineherd
gaping at the meadow?
                    Had he dreamed
the earth had opened, closed,
his herd gone squealing down
along with her,
                    the fairest flower?

What could he do but wait,
and learn, maybe, that flowers spring
from rotting flesh.

                    ★

She will come back (they said),
the sweet, red seed is on her tongue,
she will return
and we will taste her words.

                    And when she rose,
she will descend (they said)
she will descend again,
and rise
          there is no end,
spring air returns,
the birds repeat their calls,
the wind of winter wails
in trees and round the house
the same old song

               no end

                    no end

He looked (the squeal
still ringing in his ears)

275

and every thing
              everywhere
spoke to him of her

She was the water and the fish,
the stream within the stream
becoming flesh,
she was the black grain and the bread,
the wet clay and the pot,
the light, the dark,
the silence and the word,
she was all formless
on the verge of form, and form
becoming formlessness.

And so he tasted on his tongue
the song
and sang it to a lute
made from his flesh and bone

and wrote it in the clay

              no end

                     no end

5 IMAGINING WALES

GUESTS OF SILENCE

1 *Above Tintern*

Sheer above the river, cliffs.
Stroke upon stroke the current
cleaves rock.
Water builds as it breaks.
Tall above cliffs, trees.

276

Wrinkled like the mother
first imagined in stone,
an ancient face that is not
for one moment the same.

Now it looks up
and is eaten away: a gargoyle
made of water, spouting.
Vortex. Whirl of galaxies.
Circle on circle
shatters and shapes.

                    Ripple,
dint in armour
of black-bright scales.
Mailed crusaders lie in the long bed
silvery-dark.
History is a shadow roughing
the smooth skin.
Bubbles of air and light.

Glaciers crawl down the valley.
Lava erupts through a crack in the earth
and bears down, down.

The river is full
and still has room for the sky.

Lines and nets of grass
hang tangled from branches.
And the river is itself a tree
growing along the ground,
bark-ridged,
feeding with millions of leaves.

Cold, winter-blue.
Alder-green under floodmarks.

Mud colours, a sheen
of red earth.

                Suddenly
a coin of light
minted this moment,
a stroke of shadow.

So the world's likeness
appears on the canvas,
and washes out.

Crumbled and carried down,
the red earth is Adam's clay.
A wallowing mudbank
is the beached ark.

The water-face waits
desolate
for the shadow of the dove.

               Such bareness
water is, a truth
too slippery-quick to grasp,
skin-taut and bodiless
spirit, and to the poet
who comes despairing of his mind
a companion
that murmurs of the source
and infant spring,
and flows with him, and is his life.

The river fattens the lowlands
with silt, gurgles
to plainchant, whispers
under aisles raised on green lees

to the god of light.

Such sad music
the human ear shapes,
hearing in the one flow
sighs of a multitude
falling one by one.

Otter and water-rat dive,
shaped to rhythms that slip
the word-knot,
the quaver.

So bare,
yet utter.
Channel of word and song.

Water from mountain-
mother of rivers,
fleet daughter,
breaker and builder
of the parent ground.

Sweet-salt self
cleaving and raising,
sheer below cliffs
stroke on stroke
the river is

2 *At the Polish Scout House*

The house on the hillside
looks into Wales. It is fragile,
a matchwood ark, between
the beech woods and the Wye.

Yet it is we who are shapes
of air through which leaves drift
and the river runs; guests
of the silence our noise does not break.

In her shrine
the Virgin prays for her people.
She remembers Monte Cassino
and the Polish dead. At her back
autumn in the English wood smells
sweet. Leafmould heaps up
on the coverts of Katyn.

What hides from us in rooms
painted with her colour,
blue as the November sky?
Our feet brush floors rubbed bare
by the tread of regiments; heroes
whose names we cannot pronounce
look down on us from the walls.
Silence lives in the rooms we fill
with emptiness, where we drift
leaf-light in a current of air.

3 *The white wind*

Brother, did you too know
the white wind, the sudden
violent wind that streams
downriver from the hills?

Or did you at holy office hear
a sigh, a sound of wings, a song
at one with the song of love?
Or see Christ's dear blood
stream in the stained glass
where now the wind drives through?

Would we know each other
soul to soul, you who knelt
at Calvary, world's centre
within these walls, and I
who stand in the dirt nave
open to the sky?
I do not think so – only now

I feel close to you, under
the white wind from the hills
which blasts cold and downpour
through the shell, the ruin
raised on all that is broken,
the house that is always to build.

VARIATIONS ON A THEME BY WALDO WILLIAMS

Beth yw gwladgarwch? Cadw ty
Mewn cwmwl tystion.
('What is love of country? Keeping house
amid a cloud of witnesses.')

1 *Bryniau Presely*
for Susan and Huw Jones

Fire was first,
surging out of the earth.
Then the flux,
the molten stream
cooling.

And the stone stood,
intruding,
weathering.

281

On Carn Meini
it spoke to them:
blue stone,
sacred to the earth
and the fire within the earth.

Manhandled,
shaped, hauled by water
and dragged over land,
lifted up,
the stones stand,

circles,
silent tongues.

★

Or say it was by sea
the pattern was woven – skin boats
navigating along sea-boards
that would be known one day
as Brittany and Cornwall,
Ireland and Wales,
drawing together the stones,

tracing the loops and knots
of an intricate design.

It was by way of a long haul
and the energy that creates
the stone circle,
the upland pasture,
language that knits the kin,
and over all,
deeper than the sky,
durable as rock,
the invisible roof and walls.

How long does it take,
how many thousands of years,
to prepare the eternal moment?

On a day when the curlew returns,
its cry circling the moor,
suddenly, to the man
in love with time, the whole land
is the poem he will never write,
birth cry, love song, threnody
woven in voices of the living
and voices of the dead.

★

The history that he reads
is written in the land.
Its words are:
    capstone
    ogham
    Celtic cross.

Its syntax is the serpent
of the river coiling
between walls of rock.
It is homely; it moves
between neighbours
working in the fields,
in their silence, in their talk.

The history that he reads
is written in the sky:
warplanes; marks
of a slavery that imprisons him,
a man who is free.

★

Loss, surely, is part of it,
loss and despair.

Does he think sometimes
that the building is finished:
a labyrinth that no one can enter,
a house of the dead?

Or does he feel
the touch of dead hands
on monolith or carved cross?
Or hear in the silence
voices that speak of their time,
their loss?

Already the new ground crumbles,
shifts under foot –
the bishop's palace, empty as a cromlech,
the cathedral, shaken by a sonic boom.

The story is not finished,
and will not be, unless
metaphors cease to carry meaning,
the fountains of symbol run dry.

It is still the eighth day
where he walks on the hills,
a witness among witnesses,
a maker among carpenters of song.

2 *Ebbw Vale*
for Lee Grandjean

1
Tongues of fire
that transformed the earth,

joined it in iron circuits –
what have they left?

Three ponies graze
on a green field
above the valley.

These, and an old post
with strands of rusted wire,
keep out despair.

2
If there are spirits
they are like the trees
on the mountainsides
whose shape is the struggle to grow.

Iron did not master them.
Still they burn, over the seared
and dross-hard ground:

shocks of black, windblown flame.

3
What word will you carve
to speak for the dead
and not dishonour them
who forged a new world in the heart?

If there are sounds
they are valley voices,
twined with the turns of the wind
and the falling stream.

When silence fell
on the last hammer-blow
what remained in the air
but a strand of their song?

4

If there are witnesses
the wind blows through their mouths,
rain pricks their eyes
as it dints the mountain pond
which was once a mine.

And around them weathers circle,
as the high buzzard turns,
drifts and falls,
and the far ridge crumbles away.

5

What do they see but defeat?

Eyes that have watched so long
see violence woven with hope.

When all has been blown away
what lasts is a twisted flame.

3 *Strata Florida (1)*
for Wynn Thomas

They did not believe in the world
yet they built one, drawing a line
from the centre to the margins:
from Citeaux and the vineyards of Burgundy
to the Welsh uplands.

Rhys Prince of Wales granted them land:
champaign, arable, mountain pasture,
for the cure of his soul
and the souls of those before him
and the souls of those still to be born.

They expected the world to end,
and it did, not once but several times –
by fire, by dissolution.

At last almost nothing remained
of the visible structure –
stubs of walls, foundations,
a doorway open on clouds, hills.

On the surface, there is little
to speak of the makers – monks,
abbots who were patrons of poets,
princes who set aside the sword,
lay brothers who cut down woods,
built roads, tended flocks of sheep.

Only bare tombstones,
and slabs carved with a cross,
fragments of knotwork:
relics of the great design.

And near the yew that was full-grown
six hundred years ago
when a fellow poet honoured him,
Dafydd ap Gwilym lies.
Old then, the yew is ancient now,
hollow, but still alive –
no ruin, Dafydd's tree,
but rooted in and out of time,
in court song and creation's prime,
in love that every moment makes the world.

4 *Strata Florida (2)*
for M

Hawthorn and rowan and outcrop rock
above us, and an autumn breeze
fluttering your hair,
your red hair, your grey hair.

What did I mean to say
taking you there, walking
among the tombs and hart's tongue fern,
looking into the love poet's yew,
the forest of branches?

Hawthorn and rowan burning
against rock on the hills around us
and your fair fluttering,
your grey hair, your red hair,
which the wind blew into flame.

5 *Imagining Wales*
for Emyr Humphreys

A peal of thunder, a fall of mist.
Afterwards the sun glares, staring on emptiness.
It ignites an image of fire
on ashen hearths, paints
evacuated rooms with streaks of red,
stains the ruined stronghold
on the promontory.

The machines are shrouded.
The quarries sink deeper
under the shadows of their walls.
The mineshaft is a dwelling for bats.

The man sits on the mound
and stares at his hands.
He turns them over, reads the lines on his palms.

He sleeps and his dream is a coracle
in which he is tossed on a stormy sea
that has drowned the cantrefs.
He peers out, into the spray
that stings his eyes,
and gradually, out of the waters,
a mountain takes shape.
He bows his head over his hands.

He is walking alone on the shore
but is not alone.
He kicks over wrack, examines the guillemot
that flaps like an oiled rag in the wash,
the beached seal with a hole in its side.
He wanders alone thinking of the broken walls,
the silence leaking in,
the men and women who sit staring
at the backs of their hands.

What can he do that they will remember?

He knows that memory is a place
that can be lost, though it lose nothing;
a place where all things remain
to be imagined anew.

He sits on the mound alone
and looks at the lines on his palms.

He sleeps and his dream is a coracle
in which he listens, listens hard
against the crash of waters
storming round and past — listens

where there are no words,
no symbol, no metaphor
to bear him over the torrent,
nothing but courage, and his mind
that listens, listens hard
against the fall of silence
crashing round and past . . .

A peal of thunder, a fall of mist.
Afterwards the sun appears
travelling on its daily round.
The man sits on the mound
and looks at the lines on his palms.

'THAT TREES ARE MEN WALKING'
A poem dedicated to David Jones

Dry-mouthed, in a dry time,
the polluted summer air grey,
I sit down to write a poem
I have been contemplating
for twenty years – an elegy.

And find nothing,
nothing to say
about death. For
the man who died is alive,
his images flow
in the channel that he made.

Yet there is a story to tell.

It begins with a bear,
a bear that the boy sees
in a London street,

a muzzled bear,
held on a chain,
a bear which he draws, dancing.

It is a story about a bear,
and about a boy who becomes a soldier.

A bear in a London street.
A soldier caught in a tangle
of barbed wire, torn khaki
exposing his private parts,
a human being in a place
that he shares with rats,
mules, shattered trees,
dead men,
trees that are men walking.

*

The artist mixes his saliva
with the pigment,
and spits on the cave wall.

It is not himself he paints,
but the living creatures.
But he is there, at one
with the herds that flow across the wall.

No doubt of it, no doubt at all –
he makes himself at home.
There he is, too, a figure
moving across the heavens –
the bear, and the hunter of the bear.

*

A ruffled air.
A closing among the trees,
the crucked branches fallen still.

Who was sitting there in his place?
(He was a child, but that was ages ago,
before the spit dried on the rockface.)

Whose scratch marks?
Whose pawprints?

Was it Artio, mother
of the Bear who rules the Honey Isle?

Trust him to recall the names,
more than the names,
this man of courage
who descends into the hades of oblivion,
who will leave none to perish.

Does Artio wake in the cave,
or is her body the cave
from which we issue,
emerging to read the scratch marks,
follow the pawprints,
going with care over the forest floor,
penetrating the tangle,
learning to dance?

★

Grandfather Bear

        who gave his bones to the altar
        his flesh to feed the tribe
        his skin to clothe the being
        who shifts his shape,
        becomes the bear
        who dances

Mother Bear

> who digs under the roots,
> makes herself a bed,
> licks her paws, sleeps.
> When she emerges, it is spring;
> her cubs blink about her.
> She licks them into shape.

Brother Bear

> in a London street,
> brown bear on a chain,
> which the boy draws – dancing.

★

At Capel, in love
with the shape of things:

Dai, in his army greatcoat,
framed in a window, engraving.
Or walking with his friend
to unblock the stream
and free the waters.

Rhythm echoes rhythm
for the hunter of forms –
hill-shapes, trees,
hart's-tongue fern,
the horses that return
without riders –
the men betrayed to death.

Falling waters loose,
bind and loose,
shaping the ways of change.

And mist – mist crumbles rock.
Cloud packs hunt the hills.

Clouds, and mist, and something
that is neither,
a story of change woven
around the things that change.

That the dead men lie down
in the shattered wood,
shed their skins like snakes,
crawl back to the womb that bore them.

★

I paused by Nant Honddu,
by the dingle where David had a cell.

It was an enchanted place,
but what I saw was no dream.

The waters are dying, the trees
are being torn from the ground,
silt builds up in the rivers of the world,
the Thames, where he floated
the ark of his imagination,
the Rhine, the Danube
and the effluent of Europe,
the Brahmaputra,
the Nile, the Ganges,
the Euphrates, where Eden
is a desert of smoking wells.
We are making another earth;
the creatures we drew from the rock
are going back, fading,
their rhythm a distant beat.

Before the figures of the dance turn to stone,
before there is no voice left
to tell the story of the serpent
coiled around the mountains,
the serpent of drought
that Indra slew, freeing the waters,
before there is no hand to draw the bear,
no one to tell the wonder tale
of the bear waking in the cave,

pray for us, Dafydd.
David the Waterman,

pray for us.

1 GROUNDWORK

WORKPOINTS

Norfolk in April drought:
a cracked land.

Where do we begin?

Just here, say, at the point
in the fields where you see
the pinnacles of Salle church rise,
and Cawston, the naked stub
of the tower,
and the roofs of Moor Farm.

Just at this spot,
standing in a field
near the barn-studio
where oak trunks
are delivered, hitting
the brick floor with a 'dumb' sound
that pleases you.

Here, in a land of angels
carved from wood, and angels
sculpted in stone.

★

We begin at the end
of the story,
in millennial light.

Overhead on these clear April nights
the Comet's tail streams in the solar wind.

It is as if someone has opened a door
from which a light shines out
across the sky,
and into our minds
illuminating for an instant
images that have made us,
world on shattered world

and all around nebulae
are giving birth to stars.

★

Once more the visitor's book
confesses to a pilgrim
on the track of rumour, someone
who has come here seeking
the grave of Anne Boleyn.

SUNT LACRIMAE RERUM

The old song
would have us sing again
in throats that new song chokes.

★

The dull mind rises to truth
through that which is material.

Or when the mind is an image
of day without shadow,
no breeze to lift dust from the fields
or carry a seed to some moist place,
when you say to yourself
              I am this Thing,

300

this immovable block,
       and feel the weight of it
       and after a day of this,
       or a week, or a year,
             shake
yourself, and with a laugh,
shatter the thought, and,
brushing off the splinters,
              step out

        ★

How many times
the plough has gone through
the soil,
sped deep
in flinty loam

Christ alive
raised on
Adam's dust,
earth grassed
     seeded
        cropped

Word wrought in stone,
carved in wood,

don't you feel sometimes,
like an exhalation from dusty soil,
a sigh from all the acres,
all the depressions, and pits,
and pressing down of churches,
farm buildings,
don't you feel

the utter weariness of the dead?

        ★

301

What she said was:
God is nearer to us
than our own Soul:
for He is Ground
in whom our Soul standeth.

A green man pushed his head
out of the stonework, mouthing.
Angels and dragons flamed in the skies.

Shapes of belief
are still manifest
in empty niches,

makers
and image-breakers
show their hands.

★

In millennial light
wreckage
of an idea
littered on farmland
on concrete highrise
city dust and detritus

Millions becoming
one

Bones & blood
reassembling
a giant
blank-eyed

★

A day's work
is about to begin

under cross-beams
and rafters, in a space
once filled by horse-drawn carts
bringing hay or corn
from the fields.

Old iron things lie
in a corner – wheels,
parts of a ploughshare.
A rusted scythe hangs on the wall.

Oak trunks
partially shaped
stand on the floor.
Blades of light
flash down on them
like blazing swords.

★

What I want to argue
is that poetry and sculpture
are life sciences.

It is not that we express
some finished
or constructed self.

The point is to step out
into the space between

★

I like the face of this
theoretical physicist
which appeared
                an abstraction
from an unknown and undefinable
totality

and has vanished
leaving us a theory –
a theatre –
in which we sense the whole

Shall we say, though,
a molecule of carbon dioxide
that crosses a cell boundary
                    into a leaf
suddenly *comes alive*
and a molecule of oxygen
released to the atmosphere
suddenly *dies.*
Or shall we regard
life itself
as belonging
to a totality.

                    ★

The man in the mirror is no one.
                    He must get out,
stand in front of the block
                    that is not himself,
wood that has its own ways,
that will take the shape he carves,
but retain its own nature.

                    And in time
it will split, fissure,
shake the object he has made
which is not himself
and no longer a block of wood
but a thing that stands between

                    ★

Or take words – Take words!
Words that run all ways,

           spiderlines
which are at best a torn web,
or congealed in ice that freezes
heart and mind,
           snowfield
pure of the faintest print,
in which, at the first step,
the dead will come dancing
and singing from their mounds.

★

Speed the Plough
But no one now except
a solitary man driving a tractor
turns the soil
which lies folded in ridges,
dumb,
           bearing
mute trees,
church towers
foundering in the stillness
that has fallen on the land.

Stone angels stand on parapets
commanding gulfs of blue sky
and crumbling cloud.

Wooden angels stretch
in the hammerbeam roof,
each feather sensitively
carved alive,
but no one now to kindle
to imagined flight, swooping
like gulls in the wake of the plough

★

We do not deceive ourselves
that we are survivors
of an Age of Faith

or that searching for ground
is a metaphor
for meaning carried over

or that the blank page
is anything but blank

In millennial light
the ground is unimaginable

In what image can we make a shape?

Friendship, love, the self
gone out from the self

the man who has renounced power,
the woman who has assumed it,
                    and let it go

The face in the mirror is no man's –
but someone has wandered out
and stands in front of the block,
someone who is,
you say, a wonderer

CITY WALKING (1)
for Roy Fisher

There is a looking that is
a kind of touch,
                    a fingering
beyond the body's reach.

Near Paddington,
complexity of softly
growing cloud against
a builded concrete edge.

A giant's range
but we are small enough
among the press,

walking
       reaching out.

★

Between Edgware Road
and Liverpool Street,
in a cutting:
      buddleia,
a jungle of purple flowers
sprung from London brick.

★

A wind blows under Exchange House,
below steel arch and lit offices.

It blows from an older London,
out of undercuts and passageways,
across abraded façades
and worn York paving,
through railway bridges.

It plays on
work-in-progress
on a steel skeleton,
cranes reaching high,
and, glistering,
the fuselage of a jet.

★

This place, you tell me,
is your idea of world
as it will be after you have gone.

But wind still blows round
the high buildings
of black glass and steel.

And here, tangled from his fall,
is a sculpture of one more hero
who tried to fly to heaven.

★

The brown Thames laps against timbers.

A fragment of Roman wharf
is bound against a pillar,
ancient water-worn wood
against carved stone.

Inside St Magnus Martyr
splendour
of Ionian white and gold.

I listen for the music
that the poet heard.
From memory, I piece
the fragments of a song.

★

Passing where the boat went down,
it was not your dream you told me,
or mine, but I had to follow,
                          down.

Man out of air, choking.

How slowly death comes,
though it was minutes since he stood,
glass in hand,
charming and enchanted.

A sleeper on a bench
beside the river, struts
digging in his side,
turns restlessly
as the half-dead man
who dreamt that he was drowning
pops up, seal-headed, the city
with its millions of feelers
ready once more to take him in.

★

For indeed it is everywhere death
that uncovers its plague-pits
and ashes and unclaimed corpses.

Death and the desire
that clasps us in the press
or shoots us full of glances
or holds us water-mouthed
in front of images that consume.

Ebb tide reveals where London has crumbled.

Things once animate with use
are sheer matter, glutinous, unshaping:
brick, plastic, iron, rope, wire;
granite sets of a causeway,
ground down, washing away.

London on London
sunk in Thames mud.
                        Yet each set
is also a way for the vagrant mind.

                    *

Red, purple, lilac,
hand-crafted, laid:

the beauty of brick,
brittle,
                crazed.
Haunted.

                    *

Walking between the New Globe
and the river, I think of the old man
and the son who leads him,
on the Dover Road,
bringing him to the edge
of a high cliff, from which he jumps.

What an imagined fall!

Walking in the city that is continually
being made and unmade,
I think of the cliff
which Edgar built of words,
and his father's leap,
down,
        down . . .

                    *

310

To see
                    by way of words.

Stile and gate,
horse way and foot path.

Do you hear the sea?

Here's the place.

                    ★

The poet's river glides by
or oozes stickily under the wall.

It is also what exists
in the eyes of a cormorant
perching on a floating platform
above Westminster Bridge.

                    ★

The old man
is full of stories.

In this place,
Julius Caesar's men
waded across the river,
and Saxons built a church
on what was then an island
of hard gravel, washed
by the river and surrounded
by miles of marsh.

The same from whose soil
Catherine Boucher's family
made their market garden –

Catherine, who in this church,
married William Blake.

And here (our guide shows us
the vestry window) Turner
sat to paint clouds
and sunsets over the water –

where we can see tower blocks,
luxury flats, a marina,
a power station
that drives the Underground.

The old man too was married here,
twice; and his daughter
was christened, and wed . . .

As he talks, the empty church
fills silently with shadows.

It is a relief, then,
to walk on the shore
under the churchyard wall,
and look at houseboats, geese
in the water, and watch a tug
powering upriver, drawing
a barge with containers of waste.

At Battersea Bridge,
a heron flies over, mirrored
in a building of steel and black glass.

★

All in the head
so to speak,
the sacred head –
            other world
by which this world lives.

Offerings to the river-god,
father of many parts,
many changes:

a horned helmet,
a bronze shield.

Centuries will flow over them,
silt accumulate,
city on city
stand
            changing shape.

                        ★

Excavations
for power lines,
office blocks.

A head of Mithras,
traces of temple walls,
bull and bear bones,
human bones.

Voices out of air,
imagined air,
becoming vessels,
houses, journeys
underground.

                  ★

The city is also lives we do not lead.

In the Kyoto Garden,
a beautiful woman with red hair
walks elegantly, alone,

and in the time it takes her
to pause on the stone bridge
under the cascade,

we have become lovers, although
she will never know who I am
or how much damage we have caused.

★

Upstairs, in the front seat
of a bus, streets and houses
swinging round us, acacia branches
brushing the glass,
I see you: a boy
kicking a stone, playing
on bomb sites, fingering
a stone in your pocket:
looking, feeling the edge
of a concrete building
against softly growing cloud.

★

You tell me not to look back
until we are high
on Primrose Hill, turning
to see a scattering
of small lights, black
middle distance, and behind,
in a wide arc, towering blocks,
the shell of St Paul's,
far at the back

314

Canary Wharf,
a luminous triangle
in the sky.

A greeny grey phosphorescence
in lit windows conceals
unimaginable lives.
Over all, one sound –
a constant hum –
absorbs our words.

Sharp and bright
above petrol dusk
the evening star.

SEVEN SONGS

City Walking (2)
for Sarah Hemming and Julian May

Today I imagine her walking,
seven months pregnant, resting
from the effort of working with her husband,
in their terraced house in Old Woolwich Road,
preparing a room for the baby.

Down narrow brick lanes she wanders,
past iron bollards, like cannons stood on end,
behind her the Royal Observatory on the hill,
across the river, on the Isle of Dogs,
Canary Wharf gleaming, dominating the sky.
And here are gantries, industrial chimneys,
almshouses, immaculate in the shadow
of a power station with dirt-white, peeling walls.

Through a gate at Highbridge Drawlock,
down a slipway, onto a shore of shingle
and sand, where she stoops, fingering
shards of pottery and brick,
glass jewels, among the stones.

Low waves flop over,
swirl round a rowing boat swinging on a rope.
Sunlight glitters in millions of eyes.

It is peaceful here, the city
is a distant rumble; traffic,
railway, power station, refinery,
corn mill, voices – all one sound.

I let my mind move with hers over the water,
past seaweedy, green walls and piles,
converted wharves, leisure complexes,
docks, offices to let, stone church spires,
past woodwork, ironwork, ladders
descending into the water.

Today she is in love
with the city and the river,
joining and dividing, flowing through.
Silently she recites the names of bridges:
Tower Bridge London Bridge Southwark
Blackfriars Waterloo,
her mind drifting
until she sees a heron on the deck of a rusting barge
and the sight fixes her.

Sunlight in millions of eyes
glittering on the surface, through which she sees
the water's body, and feels
the channelled weight, the wild
and voiceless mother tongue.

I would follow if I could, out of the sight
of fixed and finished things, power
and after-images of power;
out of the city fractured
and constructed – the city
that is not one, but shaped to millions of needs.

For a moment only I think she enters
the place where no one can dwell,
the dark tide that generates,
pushing into gaps and inlets, carrying
driftwood, silt,

and emerges, rested, strolling home.

Before the Day Set Hard

In sleep, I cried –

I was a story that was being told,
a fugitive that fled with bleeding legs
and felt a hot breath on my neck
and on my back the thwack of staves.

I ran and ran but could not move.
My body was a beaten bush,
in which I hid, a tiny bird.

And woke. Or seemed to wake,
sleep's waters parting as I felt for ground.

And now I walked in fields above the sea,
a place of furze and granite tombs,
each Cyclops-cave an eye of dark.

And there I saw the Sun in Majesty,
which melted as I watched,
a molten rain that fell in gold drops on the sea,
and cloud that mushroomed into space,
and turbulence of cloud,
a chalice spilling poisons on the earth.

Where I looked west,
the salt fields of the deep
were Lyonesse, and palaces
of tangled wrack, and leaping rocks
were dolphins turned to stone,
or submerged effigies of ancient knights.
And overall a wounded tanker
wallowed, bleeding oil.

I walked upon the cliffs
and heard a small bird sing,
a jingle and a trill which rose and fell,
a strident churr.

Don't ask or seek to know, a voice said then.
The story being told is what you are.

I trod the waters of a dream,
and reached for ground, and heard
the strange voice say:
You are a woman at the door of time.
Imagine, then, anew.

Then in a dark-mouthed tomb,
a Cyclops-eye, I saw an eye,
a tiny, bright and living thing.
I saw a cocked-tail flit,
and sensed, so near, a clutch
of breast-warm eggs which nestled
in a globe of moss and down.

So near, before the day set hard –
    but must it set?

Or shall I tell the story as I choose,
and walk on cliffs above the main,
and see the sparks of furze, and feel with her,
the hunted bird that dwells in caves,
the bird who makes her nest inside the tomb?

Cyane
Finally a body that is water's own.

So at times words seem to come to me,
as though I could speak,
or as I remember speaking in another life.

I pool to a glassy stillness.
I move slowly, mirroring
shapes & colours of leaves;
housefronts, walls; a face;
the world entranced
gazing at the world.

Or quick, a stream
of silver – only
what I know is imageless,
except once, in another life . . .

My moods are stagnant,
turbulent. I circle circle circle,
or stand motionless, or pour out,
falling, scattering,
coming together with the smoothness
of a dolphin's back, an icy glide.

What was I before I was finally this?
Sometimes I dream that on my surface
I form a human face,
and look out at another,
red and glistening, a man's,
and arms, in which he grasps a woman,
binds her to him, drags her down.

And it shakes then: earth quakes,
and springs apart – they are gone.

And I shake, the being that I was –
              skin blood bones
unbinding, flying into drops,
flowing with a constant tremor,
plunging down, shattering,
shaking out long and smooth,
always broken, always whole.

And over I go and over,
and under, and round and round.

But what is that but a dream
that I was human once,
who am pure spirit,
not bodied, not bodiless,
but water in water, quick
with a life beyond all words.

Silence, then; or a voice
that is the sound of water running,
in which, if they listen,
any one may hear a tale
of terror at the roots of things:

a tale that I tremble to tell,
half remembering, or inventing,
but as if, once, it were my own.

Land's end

'. . . in the sea nothing lives to itself.'
        Rachel Carson

She has saved her body from the sea
once more, but feels engirdled still,
tangled with wrack,
bound with straps of kelp
whose loose ends slap her legs
as once again she clambers up the shore
and feels beneath her feet
the final grains of sand,
the hidden matrices.

So consciousness returns.

But as her head emerged from webs of foam,
sleek in the swell,
                what had she seen?
Rock stacks, sheer falls,
chance balancings of rock on rock;
rock flattened, rounded,
scooped out, split,
                a spectacle
of camelbacked and giant shapes,
ribbed matter historied and named,
headland pharos and the chambered tombs . . .
Then – closer – quartz
and crystal sparkle, mica shine,
the sun a blade laid on the sea.
And, in a stroke of dark,
the meltdown world,
Plutonic depths,
the serpent fire, long cooling
that no mind can see,
the blank face of the rock.

And what she sees is blank.
Earth an island made of cloud,
no ground, but everywhere –
ghost sun in mist –
a bone mask showing through.

But what is this?
Half fish, half woman, carved in wood,
a man's embodied knowledge
in the cutting touch,
a feel of salty flesh –
which she stands looking at,
and hears windrush of breaking waves
and feels again the labour
of the tide,
and then the long pull out
beyond land's end,
as she takes leave,
at liberty to ride the deep,
and once more save her body from the sea.

Between Worlds

Earthbound, she thinks; all power
gone into the ground –

And if any soul could come back now
and find me in their place?

Outside, she sees a wild man
with a club held across his chest.
And here are angels – they are scaly,
and might be mermaids, but
the scales are armour – warriors,
their wingtips pointed, like fern.
Old gods and the young god

and his cohort –
                        and one visitor
with her hand on the latch.

Inside, tall pew ends catching
her sight are, momentarily,
a large congregation.
Space releases her spirit,
which a familiar musty smell brings down.

If any soul could return, moving
invisibly between worlds,
and meet her
where she stands,
not questioning, but a question
to herself . . .

But here is no one,
and if there were,
how desolate the soul finding her;
how dank with the tears of things,
damp-spotted stone,
emptiness.

No one. Then, for an instant,
she feels fury frozen
into wood and stone; fury
in niches
violently emptied,
statues flung down,
faces smashed.
Through plain glass she can see
wind streaming, lifting grass over graves.

And now, walking away,
it is as though the wind
were shaping all she sees –

curves of the land
and dark, wooded hollows,
whirlpools among wheat,
stone angels on the roof
                    flying.

In her eyes filled by the wind
the tower is an island
in a blue gulf, and she
is a leaf blown from a twig
and whirled away.

Groundless She Walks

Her footstep strikes
the dusty track.
                    Heat-haze
on ripening wheat creates
a shimmer in which the gorged pigeon
flaps away losing shape.
In dark places, in their own spheres,
minute creatures webbed in moisture
vibrate at her burdened tread.
And she feels down through cracked earth,
knowing something about them, sensing
the rhythms by which they live.
And what, she thinks, are their constellations,
what gods burn in their heavens?
Do they too know a Cassiopeia who holds up her arms?
Are they companioned, or unsupported
except by physical law,
sheer materiality, lumpen as flints
which will indifferently turn my ankle
or break a plough?
                    Instability
was the mark of the day when she woke.
She has been at the edge

since first light crazed mirror and window glass,
froze the lightning of the garden tree
against the toppling tidal wave of earth.
She is a woman carrying a child who flinches
at the momentary thought she is a man
who dreams herself to be a woman,
and who now is walking beside a harvest field,
kicking up the dust,
                    alone, afraid.

What is possible? she insists, feeling
again the movement under her heart.
                    Who was it said
'the march of time'?
Months weeks days hours minutes seconds
hard boots striking sparks from flint
regiments tramping from the cave-mouth
                    down the years.
And must it be so, faces
with the same blind look ever
appearing, disappearing – one likeness
dominant as Jupiter in the night-sky?

An obstruction in the flow: blackness
shot through with flashes of light,
scintillations,
her mind itself the sky
in which a woman lifts up her hands
over heavy-headed wheat,
the whole sea of the field whispering.

But she may not dissolve;
she must absorb turbulence;
the desire within to be other
is the pressure she must bear.

But must the story repeat itself,
the flame be kindled to burn as one
with the whole fire that consumes and dies?
Let me take a seed of thought
and find for it a cryptic niche,
some damp place under soil or under bark,
a home of bacteria, of creatures
that live in water, and grow there
a being that moves to another rhythm . . .

But now her mind is an ice-berg
in a polar sea, mountainous dark
moving under her, bearing her along.

And instantly the image fractures,
and dissolves.

What, then, is possible? she cries
silently, as groundless her footstep
strikes the dusty track.

The child I carry
will crawl into the world.
What ground will he stand on?
What humus, or piece of debris
hurtling from the supernova,
the giant star that once was man?

The Seventh Song

'Life is what we never see.'
Michel Henry

**The seventh song
is groundlessness.**

Born out of language
it came, as though a poem
were a bloody birth,
its mother more than words.

Fingering a stick,
rounding the hand to a hold, it came.
Stick that digs in a ditch.
You know who it is that digs, making a hole.

But what is this? Noise of traffic
out there. In here
you go right down, you reach
into the smell of the hole, soil
tickle-whiskering your face.
In here you go right down to a place
that is not the world.

Other sounds, too, make
the seventh song.
Crump
of bombs, mosquito whine
that belongs with the roughness
of blankets, under ground,
recoil of the guns
that rock your cradle,
and the Welsh gunner's tenor voice,
which you hear only
because you were told about it,
singing in the field.

What you loved most was touch:
the feel of earth: dark crumbs
on which the spirit feeds.
In that sense
the way leads back, into chalk,
into earth that is humped, mounded,

into stone dwellings where they sit
in their birthday skeletons,
with their hand-axes
and ornaments made of animal teeth.

Bullrush gravel-pit waters
rise in the mind. Without these,
without the first Moses-basket,
there would be no seventh song.
And there is that, that only,
a boy-girl feeling no one can ever see.

There is what the flow is made of:
scribbles on a wall,
a note left on a pillow,
indecipherable,
written to say:
I have gone to see the world.

And there you are: on the sea-wall,
having crapped and wiped your bottom
with a handful of grass,
and now running up and down
waving a piece of seaweed.

               Without this,
there would be no seventh song.

What it sings is a way,
a growing that is a growing round.
As seasons are in wood,
present tissue –
                 that day
in wartime, babies in a pram,
cousins, a boy and a girl; the sun
that enters under the coverlet,
revealing nothing but itself,

pavement over which the wheels bump –
nothing that is any more
than what it is felt to be.

Or footsteps where shingle moves,
time in time that can be seen,
almost,
        sift of tiny pebbles,
shells, infant green carapaces,
evacuated of life.
But it cannot be seen in these,
nor in water that eats the substance
out of sea-walls, water
that moves, laps, flows.

However fluent, it cannot be seen
in the song, nor in this or that,
the hole or the digging stick,
the place down under,
in this world,
which you would learn one day
to call the Antipodes.

**The seventh song
is groundlessness.**

But it is here, look,
in your hands,
which are perfectly empty.

FROM DEBRIS: A CYCLE OF POEMS

*From debris
of collapsing stars,
from gas and dust,
where nothing is wasted,
a stream of images.*

Ground-Ivy

Hobnailed
imprinting the soil,
Adamah stops,
bound to the spot,
wondering at the tiny
smoke-blue flower
that bears his mother's name.

Night Piece

Cut of farm roofs, black
against sunset,

owl hoot sounding
the depth of woods:

the present is a blade
you could try with your thumb.

It is a haunting thought
that there are no ghosts,

only this black and shining edge.

Owl Country

Where the beck trails
alders and dark
feather-headed reeds,
at the foot of a post,
a pellet:
compacted fur,
yellow teeth
with which a vole
would gnaw
              no more.

Feathered Deaths

On the concrete floor,
three heaps of feathers,
pied wagtails
that found their way in.

The view through the window
seems endless, a pathway
through sky over the planet,
the flowing cloud.

Lark Song

Springing
from clod and flint

rising
invisible

or a black dot
quivering

raining over
and all around

song shower
in April air.

Lucky Strike

Returning from a raid,
just missed the tower
where, over the West Door,
the Wild Man with oak leaves
wound round his body
faces the Dragon
            wreathed in vines.

Crash landed at Church Farm,
ploughing itself in,
churning up the loam.
Two crew dead.
                    The Flight Engineer
periodically revisits
the old country, resuming
his portion of the pasture.

Angels at Salle

I feel for them:
                    spirits
bodied in stone, motionless
winged beings the wind abrades,

soldiers standing at their post
on a long-abandoned field.

Palimpsest

Hand-painted,
the stories of death
and resurrection;
in the margin,
matters of business,
manorial accounts:
fodder, grain, sheep.
Requiem eternam . . .
et lux perpetua.
Here, too, in the light
of workaday transactions
the poetry of meaning.

Magnolia

Flowers opening,
foxglove-red at base,
creamy shell-like petals

scatter your images on the ground
where the tree springs,
flowers erect,

where it moves in you
and the only word
you feel in your mouth
is **tongue**.

For Quickness

Observation (looking at the magnolia) can become an idol.

Why should seeing be painful, unless one is possessive, wanting to see all?

It is feeling with, feeling into, that respects the other.

Distance makes this possible. There is no other way of coming close.

Pastoral

A field gate,
five bars of weathered oak,
goose grass cleaving to them,

a gate stuck open
permanently,
rusted chain hanging.

Once the way
from the fields to the horse pond
in its semi-circle of ash-trees;
from the pond
to woods solid with shadow,
through woods to the church,
stone wildmen and dragons,
to labourers' homes.

You may say it opens on
a world that is dead.
I would reply that,
like the goose grass,
this is where I like to be.

Crops

Early one August morning
he inspected his crops.

In a cornfield
due to be harvested,
a rectangular shape
had formed in the dew
and with it, across his land
a legion of ghosts.

Later,
sun dried the grain
leaving only a crop
to be gathered in.

Sculptor's Workshop

We stand at the end of a long time
looking back through a telescope.

Galaxy collides
with galaxy,
a shock wave speeds out.

Inside the spiral arms
old stars are dying.

Bright in the blue ring,
from dust and gas,
stars are being born.

Not Newton

The old bramley
bowed down
under the weight
of big apples

a red admiral
feeding on
a windfall

a green woodpecker
flying away
laughing

nothing
but
energy.

Hare

Fear of us makes
the heart jump,
the body leap, the long legs
run uphill, and stand –

Absolute hare,
long ears laid back,
long skull, our image
a gleam in dark eyes.

Blackberrying: A Conversation Piece

Whether birds feel joy in their flight
Whether one's lifework might be something no one wants
Whether one will end up living in a cardboard box
Whether love is an element like air or fire
Such are the questions on their purple tongues.

Quick Dancers

Brief chaotic spirals
formed of the dust of the ground,

dancers born of wind
and loose soil

which rise, flinging
themselves into the air,

almost natural phenomena
in which you believe,

picturing rhythm
and image: breathing life

into quick dancing figures
formed of the dust of the ground.

Hogweed

Skeletal
on a hedgebank
against darkening sky

you imagine it
a wizard's wand
to conjure up the wind and snow

a telescope
to focus on
the Christmas star

a pipe
in fingers
stiff as ice
to play the New Year in.

Reading Walls

A late summer evening
darkens, light rain begins
to fall, swallows wheel
over us where we peer
at walls webbed with age
and feel with our fingers
signatures, initials,
names hand-cut in brick,
rough lines of those
who made the track
through the fields, dug clay

337

from the pit, wielded
the rusted scythe
that hangs on the barn wall
under the swallows' nests.

Earthling

How many space craft
have left for far destinations,

planetary, heavenly,
ideas carrying their cargoes

of visionary beings
who will not return.

Far-seeing, or new-born dead
in your shrouds,

I am your fellow,
strange as you are,

but let me stay, smelling
earth and pond water at dusk.

Standing Upright

Two-legged
walking
stretching
like a tree
but not rooted
like fence post
telegraph pole
but not fixed
something
with an inside

made of darkness
speaking hand
dumb mouth
closing
opening

Autumn

Spiderlines appear
in the garden overnight.

She might have spun them
herself, so carefully

she moves, taking
the whole new garden in.

Leap

Day is blown through
by a wind that scours,
a wind that reveals.

Cloud is driven over,
sky clears,
and in the instant
imagination cuts
a shape of belief.

2 DEDICATIONS

WALKING TO SLEEP
A poem for my mother

Hours before you died,
I read you once more the poem
you first read to me
in which the merman mourns
for his human wife
who has left the sea
and will not come away,
down, down, who will not come away.

Then you, whose life
had been to care and comfort,
were walking to sleep –
                walking,
counting the stones the shells
dog whelk cuttle-bone
shepherd's crown
fairy loaves anything
of interest on the shore
in sight of the Island
in sound of the sea.

Walking, walking down
where, hours before,
you heard a voice that said
'Start again, Start again'.

★

This is the shore
on which you loved to walk
in childhood, as a woman
with a family, and in age.

                    Walking
in love and in sorrow,
not looking away, but finding
in yourself the place
where you were most alone.

Walking, and always finding
something of interest –
driftwood, pulse of sunlight
in water, gull floating
on the swell.

What I think of now
is that place,
and of you watching, listening,
as I cast your ashes on the sea.

                    ★

Your father was the same,
wanting no stone to mark his life.

Was it humility, or pride?
I only know he lived in you,
as you live in me.

Here are countless stones
and on all and every one
the print of memory. . .

What can I say that is not untrue?

You gave me love of poetry,
and with it, knowledge
that words are a shore
on which one must walk to the end,
and look far out, hoping

to glimpse the thing, the being
that one loves, and must let be.

★

Ash and specks of bone,
which a breeze blows back,
making a grey smear
on dry shingle,
which the next wave covers.

Yes, the tide is coming in,
the next wave leaps farther
up the shore, sluices
the shingle as it slides.

Beyond the swash,
the tinkling, shifting stones,
a gull dives down
out of the bright, late sun
and settles on the sea – one gull that seems
to have the whole bay to float on.

★

The martins we often watched
have left again,
their holes in the cliff-face
look down where sand falls,
clay slips,
and a notice informs us
that this is an unstable place.

For you, on this bright day,
winter almost here,
no place.

Spots and patches of light
dance as the waves break.
White light,
greeny-grey water,
ash that is blown back
and waves fetch and cover.

Now, for the first time,
you who would gladly comfort,
look away.

★

What is the scent on the salt air?
I search, and find
a few late flowers:
sweet alyssum,
tiny white faces
among rocks, sea defences
of Portland stone.

Shall I lend you my senses
to know once more the finds
that every day delighted you
and bound you to the world?

I do not find you in this ash
that vanishes among the foam –

ash that is less than anything
you lingered over,
                              walking
counting pebbles shells
bladder wrack dulse
kelp with a holdfast stone.

It is not words that hold you
any more than shingle keeps
the water that sluices it,
sifts, running down,
changing its shape.

It is not you who dissolve
as I come to the edge of the shore.

A POEM FOR MY FATHER

'The first region is colour.'
H. W. Fawkner

November: a no-month grey sky
brings out the colours:
earth-red of a flowerpot in the garden,
brown soil and decaying leaves
washed fresh by rain.
The birch-tree is a yellow light
burning outside the window.

Inside, I pick over dead things:
a brush with stiff bristles,
tubes in an old paintbox,
battered and stained,
all magic gone except the names:
yellow ochre, burnt umber, cobalt blue . . .

★

Alkali or acid?
            It is knowledge
that dies with the man who knew soils,
expert on phosphate and nitrate, on mulch.
I see him in his old raincoat
fixing a garden line,
or treading down earth round the roots

344

of a young apple tree,
or pruning with a knife
curved like the horn of the moon.

He liked to say he came south
in a green winter, Yorkshire
edging his voice in the soft country.

We would hear him singing in the ward
as we came up the stairs –
death-knell of a fine baritone,
the romantic, handsome man
who liked women, single in his love.

Over his bed the painting of a cornfield
he could no longer see,
splashes of bright red,
bluish-green elms, the fullness
of summer days we could feel and smell.

★

It was fear also that he taught,
white-faced, his hand
electric in my hand – a man
hugging the wall by the stone steps,
following the hedge round the field,
crouching at the simultaneous
lightning bolt and thunder crack,
crying out,
             'Who should we help'.

        Fear and a pride
that might have been humility –
a man with Constable's
'God's gift of seeing', who avoided public view,
making his home his gallery.
        'A perfectionist,' he said,

'that's what I was' – an artist
who destroyed more pictures than he left,
who found a place out of his time,
and set up his easel by river
and in field corner
                painting
                        impossible
                                peace.

★

I have never seen a stranger thing
than his dead face,
false smile on an effigy,
an immaculate, dressed up corpse.

Outside, a downpour,
the streets of Christchurch
running with water,
the Avon racing full,
spray jetting from tyres,
leaves whirling or dancing
or plastered to the road.

I could think of nothing, only
a story he liked to tell – when
he was a young man working in Scotland,
one day, he did not go out in the boat
which was caught in a storm on the loch,
was not drowned with his two companions,
as his landlady thought,
who ran about the house crying,
'Wheer's my laddie, wheer's my bonnie laddie?'

★

Oak branches tufted with grass
mark the winter floods. On banks,
between leafless trees, yellow
of primroses, first daffodils.

In the stillness,
a woodpecker's hammer-notes vibrating.
From a wooden bridge, I scatter ash
which the current gathers,
bears down,
moving in snaking lines,
smudging dark water,
reflections of branches and sky.

*

I follow the way of the water with my mind
        flowing –
through wood and meadow,
under Boldre Bridge,
past the Shallows, where he painted
and I fished with my first bamboo,
the quick mirror-surface distorting us,
as here, it twists the trees.
      And for a time
all seems colourless,
until I look close and see again
the darkest dark that is depth
of colour – sky-and-water mix
of yellow and blue and brownish green,
the surface bark, or a nest of snakes
shedding their skins,
flicker-tongued adders of fire
dissolving in depth, the bodied
escaping appearances,
the bodiless the broken the whole
        flowing through.

*

It is the knowledge that dies,
stories one half-remembers
without the voice,
no particle of the living
reducible to an image or a word.

         In this region
there are no appearances,
no painted surfaces, only fire
that burns with the life in things.

To hold it
is like putting your fingers in a flame,
or trying to bring back an object
from a dream –
treading down firmly on the stairs of water,
rising slowly to the air.
And at the last something clutches
at your wrist and you wake scared,
hand tingling, your empty, open hand.

NOT LIKE ICARUS
for my brother David

Not like Icarus – your white legs,
your strong, man's legs,
out of the water, up in the air, waving.
And I looking on from the shore
as you stood on your hands on the sea-bed –
astonished, longing to follow.

How powerful you seemed,
how indestructible,
your crawl into the waves
a total mastery,

your disappearance
a certain prelude to return,
hands dripping with treasure.

But water was not the element you loved.

I remember the silhouettes
on your bedroom wall, the diagrams,
the balsa-wood models –
Lancaster, Heinkel, Hurricane –
all the exotic names and shapes,
as strange to me as flint axes
and mammoth bones, but to you
the romance of the real, freedom
you would learn to master.

I don't believe in your death,
you are too much part of the world
that held you, free of the air,
as I once saw you when I was a boy
and you were a young man, diving
for a handful of gravel and mud,
waving to us with your legs, surfacing.

But words were not the poetry you wanted.

I remember the excitement
with which you ran from the house
at the noise of low-flying jets,
the look of a boy on your man's face
at the far-off sound of a speck
that seemed to float in the blue.

Nothing could compare with the drone
of the engine, ground spreading out,
cloud streaming past and the sun above,
your surge into the wide, blue sky.

Then you would dip again, down
to the earth that kept you
for a time but did not hold you.

KEATS IN WINCHESTER
for Elizabeth Bewick

What should poetry make,
Keats,
of your absence?
                              Poetry
that finds every thing
every place interesting.

Here, it is your Autumn still,
though burnt stubble spreads
its blackened hedgehog skins
across the downs, and smoke
clings to walls where the house
you lodged in stood, where
you lived again Tom's death
and lived your own, while
the landlady's son scraped his violin.

When smoke clears,
when the yellow hazel leaf
closed like a tiny hand
dances on invisible silk,
there is a light within the light,
which, like a spring-tide,
floats the city off its sunken base,
and gives a grace of sail to hulks of stone.

You are no shade
in the valley of bones.

You have left no relic
where you loitered
reading a love letter,
on the cathedral floor
      sinking down
      down
      to the dead waters
               dragging down.

You have braved the dream –
the white face on the altar steps,
the fallen Titan's agony and rage.
Now it is finished –
            a fragment,
open on the desk,
as lightly you step out
through the Close, turn down
College Street, and walk
to the water-meadows,
leaving the place a living soul.

IN THE FOOTSTEPS OF NO-ONE

in memory of R. S. Thomas

After the closed door, silence.

After the death-fog, emptiness.

After the emptiness, images –

      a shape of words,
we could say,
no bigger than a man's hand,
a cloud, a flock of birds whitening
the March ploughland, blackening
mountains & moorlands & the coasts of Wales,

351

a mist rising off moist furrows
and the earthen crock of a skull
with its question-mark curl of spirit.

Who is this man
who proclaims himself no-one?
What is his boast?

Old salt, lashed to the father-tree.
Priest on his knees, daring to question
He Who Is Not At Home.
Listener with his ear to the shell
of the church that was Wales,
waiting for a worthy people.

Proud man, nobly infirm, stag
sniffing the air for a rival.
Austere old man, suddenly
skipping like a youth
to the pleasures of his lady.

As for myself, I most remember
a night when his voice refused us
everything but the poem,
which seemed to reach out,
and quavering on the air
came an owl's voice from Powys woods
seeming to answer.

So the images, the cloud,
we might say,
the flock descending
appear to settle, and rise,
as a mist,
leaving moist blades shining.

Afterwards silence
that is a different sound,
the mountains, the moorland, the sea
and the sea-watches
sharper, brighter,
and more the same than we ever knew.

Like a door, we might say,
which the man has opened,
and closed behind him,
leaving it as it always was,
but now too strangely different,
the land of a poet who dared to be human.

HARDY OF WESSEX
to Donald Davie

We go back to him,
thinking we can read his face,
like the land's –
Mr Hardy's, writer,
late of Max Gate, Dorchester.

What we want him to be, he is:
our elegist, whose heart lies
in the mould that shaped it –
from which we conjure him,
melancholy as a robin in winter
whistling on a tomb.

He is our shade, but
it is we who haunt him, walking
the dungy by-ways, shadowing
the cloud-dark Dorset heights.

Still he looks down at us,
on the road he too struggled up,
scattered with the shards of our armies,
lit by the glare of nuclear fires.
We look back, reading in his face
the stories we tell ourselves,
that are not true.

FOR A WOMAN WHO SAID SHE COULD FALL IN LOVE WITH A BOAT

for Mieke on her fiftieth birthday

What I wish you is not a sieve
or a chugging tub
or a hulk half sunk in the mud
with ribs that clutch at the sky,
but a sound bottom,
good timbers throughout
and oceans ahead to plunge in.

Or a canoe, maybe, or a kayak,
for mountain lakes and rivers,
skin or bark rider of rapids
and a wise spirit to guide you –
sickle-gleam glimpsed between cedars,
new moon drifter on dark water
                    bringing peace.
Or a rowboat,
oars dripping,
crawling in creeks – where you anchor,
and lie back, head pillowed,
and dream, rocking, rocking,
watching the sailing sky.

Or else a thoroughbred yacht,
sail taut as a fin or billowing,
gull-white hull with lines
sleek as a great northern diver –
a yacht which never dives, but cuts through waves
over the crab's den and the lobster's lair,
over stones and mud where the weeds are,
under, down under, while it races over
and ocean is its pasture.

Better for you a boat like a dolphin,
a mythical craft,
part mammal and part bird.
Nose up, nose down, and the back curves
out of the water, awash and shining.
What are you then but the sea
and the sea's daughter,
waves riding waves
and spume in your hair?

Best of all though I wish you
one of your native boats.
Not a *tjalk* with a hold
full of vegetables and household stuff,
or the floating barn of a flat-bottomed *aak,*
smelling of grain and stone to mend roads.
No grandfather barge which you would care for
like a beloved elder, retired
from the work of the world.

Rather an antique sailing boat
with brass portholes and polished timbers,
stately and playful and worthy
of every weather,
canal-wise and ocean-knowing,
a boat with an engine that never fails,
and room below when you carry a fellow voyager,
and a red sail.

THOUGHTS ON A STAR-MAP

for Lee on his fiftieth birthday

Venus bright
in the dawn sky
of your birth-month.

Jupiter and Saturn
crossing the sky
from east to west.

Think of light
travelling for a million years,
more than a million,
the astronomers' unimaginable
numbers and times,
but light which the eye sees:

Andromeda,
sister galaxy,
faint as a smudge of dust.

Think of the names
we pin on the sky. Imagine them
falling back like acid rain,
and the bright object,
without number or name,
swimming in its own light.

*

Time to begin.

A block of wood
lies on the studio floor –
a windthrown trunk
that was feathered with leaves.

New light flashes
through gaps in the roof
where lately swallows flew in,
cutting the air.

      Think of the birds
flying away. Imagine the sound
of a human kiss
waved into space.
What will it find?
Who will know what we are?

ARNOLDS WOOD
2005

A poem in memory of Les Arnold, poet and teacher

ARNOLDS WOOD

'Hopeful young trees,' we said,
as we planted them,
colleagues and friends,
digging down through matted grass.

It was a day in February.
White blossom against black sticks
in hedges, frogspawn in the farm pond.

From your home field
on the Cotswold ridge,
we could see the white horse
on the edge of Salisbury Plain.

The wind was cold, and felt like snow.

★

The names of the trees would please you:

wild cherry
mountain ash
maple apple hazel
birch
oak
lime
whitebeam
beech
walnut
hawthorn
wild pear

crab apple
guelder rose
American locust

They speak of abundance,
like William Carlos Williams,
the poet you loved best.

They too affirm a generous soil.
They will grow leaves
that shake in the wind.

★

'He was close to nature,
He inspired us.' Looking up
from a student's words,
I saw leaves on a birch-tree
dancing in the wind,
and at once, in that glance,
I knew.

The words startled me
and in the tree
shaking, swaying, dancing
I saw their truth.
It was the rhythm of joy
given and received,
which I knew in an instant,
and hope not to forget again.

★

I want to make a poem
for both of us.

Nothing rhapsodic
to make you laugh at me.

What I want to make for us
is a place in words
which we might share.

As once we planned
to work on a writing
about landscapes:
Cotswold limestone,
southern chalk.

*

Is that why thinking
about you I keep seeing walls?

Rough-textured, drystone
walls dividing fields.
Weathered, hand-marked
limestone, yellow and grey.
Chiselled, the stones
of St Laurence's
skull house, the Saxon church
where carved angels
high over the chancel arch
seem to swim in air.

In God's love, I thought.
till, peering into half light,
I saw that they are helmeted,
military guards with the job
of admitting some to heaven
and keeping others out.

Yet they were, too, figures
of energy, athletes
delighting in their element.

*

The walls are here
word on word
because I thought of you
crossing fields
gathering in sheep

Cotswold stone walls
at Leigh House Farm
where I saw you alive
and saw you dead.

★

Do we abandon the dead
by leaving places where they died?

Ask the daffodils
by the Haycombe road.

Ask the fields
of Newton Park, the stones
of the castle tower.

How should one be
here
who is nowhere?

And by what right
do I ask?

As though I could command
any spirit, or a dead man
had less right than the living
to be left alone.

★

Sometimes
it is as though things
themselves want to speak:

ancient walls, buildings,
the bridge over the Avon,
autumn ploughland,
pasture on the Cotswold ridge.
Almost, in the air and light,
        a voice.

Or perhaps it is a feeling,
even a dampness
which earth and stones exude,
and we may interpret,
calling it continuity.

But what time is it ever
for the living except the moment?

And for the dead,
this is not their place.
They are not like the stones
that speak of them.

They are not here.

                    ★

September
rain, mist-hidden
country,
all day reading
tracking you
word in word out
looking in windows

to find you
looking out
    gone

★

Sometimes in this country
cloud conspires with stone
to make a prison for the spirit.

           The man
I want to talk to is alive
in the detail of his poems.
It seems that, reading,
I could call him out, ask
whether what I am making
is a place he could inhabit.

Help me, I want to ask,
to avoid the humourless
self-importance
of middle age.

★

After hail, blue sky,
cloud drawing shadow
over fields and downs.

How thin the window seems.

The face at the window
is the wind.

★

Late September:
new students

flock to classrooms
where we see
momentarily
old faces, you
standing
arm upraised –

shepherd,
conjuror.

★

Wool caught on a thorn
tells a winter's tale
to the empty fields.

He is beside himself
transforming the stage
to a world of sheepwalks
and golden fleece.
Sheepman and wife
lying together in effigy
quiver alive.

He is telling again
the tale of things we met with
dying and new born.

★

Poet, teacher:
did it drain you
to quicken the life
in other minds?

Below me, a mallard
dives and rises, dives

and rises,
stands up in the water
shaking
in ecstasy.

★

Old stonework,
monster faces with open mouths,
for seven hundred years
the same expression
gaping & leering.

Did I think you too
belonged to the long centuries?

★

Outside,
clear evening light,
a kestrel hovering
over the young trees
we planted in your memory.

At table, it is almost
as if you neglect us.

★

Smoke from burning stubble
hangs in the air
over hill fields
towards the crematorium.

Impossible to think
of oneself as absent,
all one's roots
entangled
in the world.

★

Grief is almost
hearing a voice,
feeling
a hand on the shoulder.

Grief is words
that have to be spoken,
and are less than the air
of which they are made.

★

Shining April days,
grass greener,
sky bluer
after rain.

Daffodils wither,
dandelions open
sunfaces at the base of walls.

I have dreamt about him
again, clumsily
mentioning in his hearing
how we will commemorate him
when he dies.

★

One thing you can be sure of:
death will change our lives.

★

As we walked here
on the castle mound,
you told me you felt
you were walking
into a black tunnel.

Now the strange, delicate
pink and white cyclamen
is out by the ivied stump
where I walk between classes
to rest my mind.

It is a quiet time
when light shining on the walls
seems to fall through centuries
picking out one question:

how to shape a life.

★

In Bradford on Avon
I was startled to see you
as you were, a man with black hair
walking on the pavement.
The plane trees still
by the bridge had lost
most of their leaves. Swans
were riding the river
turbulent after rain, running
greeny-brown close to the arches.

Everything seemed to be as expected.

The man who turned
                was a stranger.

★

We get used to death.

Then one day,
suddenly,

it is incredible –
we do not believe
he will not walk in.

★

The year comes round
with a shiver.

It is the time when,
sitting at your desk,
I found among your papers
the poem of home-making
you had written for me,
and which I read then
for the first time.

Green light at my window,
rain dripping from leaves,
cold spring rain
shivering.

★

Hedgerows smoulder in mist.
Spidersilk mats rough bark
on great plane trees
beside the Avon.

Through stone streets,
between high walls,
the drift of leaves,

one year on.

★

A raw winter.

In your poems too
I find openness,
exposure.

★

To live for ever
would annihilate
everything we love.

I see we need death
somehow.

★

Dusk like nostalgia
settles outside.
December dusk,
with snow
that is now and past
falling
continuously
falling

★

The trees are still small,
but high enough to hide
all but the stone wall
canopied with ivy,
the roof and walls
of the farm.

Cloud over chalk ridge,
a man full of life
pulling a cork
pouring in our glasses
red wine.

★

The black car
that tore into silence
left a distant hum.

The world has closed
behind it, leaving
the faintest breath.

I start out to follow
plodding
on my two feet.

★

It is just possible
you will teach me
to make a friend of death.